INSTANT VORTEX AIR FRYER OVEN COOKBOOK 2020

AFFORDABLE AND DELICIOUS INSTANT AIR FRYER OVEN RECIPES FOR COOKING EASIER, FASTER, AND MORE ENJOYABLE (BEGINNERS AND ADVANCED USERS)

@Copyright 2020by Marian Spence- **All rights reserved.**

This document is geared towards providing exact and reliable information in regards to the topic and issue covered. The publication is sold with the idea that the publisher is not required to render accounting, officially permitted, or otherwise, qualified services. If advice is necessary, legal or professional, a practiced individual in the profession should be ordered.

Under no circumstance will any legal responsibility or blame be held against the publisher for any reparation, damages, or monetary loss due to the information herein, either directly or indirectly.

CONTENTS

Introduction 8
Cooking with Instant Vortex Air Fryer Oven 10
Cooking Timetable 11
FAQ: Instant Vortex Air Fryer Oven & Food 12
    How do air fryers ovens work? 12
    Is air frying a healthier food preparation option than deep frying? 12
    What foods work best in the Vortex Plus? 12
    Can I use my Vortex Plus to crisp up frozen fries and fish sticks, or pre-deep-fried chicken wings or fingers? 13
    Are there foods that cannot be cooked in my Vortex Plus Air Fryer Oven? 13
    How much food can I fit in my Vortex Plus? 13
    Do I need to preheat the Vortex Plus? 13
    What happens if don't turn my food when reminded to? 14
    What can I bake in the Vortex Plus Air Fryer oven? Do I need a special baking dish? 14
    My food is not crispy-what am I doing wrong? 14
    I have birds, is the Vortex Plus safe to use around them? 14
Breakfast and Brunch Recipes 15
    Eggs in Bread Cups 15
    Eggs in Avocado Cups 16
    Sausage with Eggs 16
    Chicken Omelet 17
    Bacon & Sausage Omelet 18
    Zucchini Omelet 19
    Bacon & Spinach Quiche 20
    Macaroni Quiches 21
    Trout Frittata 22
    Mixed Veggie Frittata 23
    Turkey & Spinach Cups 24
    Savory Carrot Muffins 25
    Sweet Potato Rosti 26
    Zucchini Fritters 26
    Oats, Nuts & Seeds Granola 27
Vegetarian Recipes 28
    Buffalo Cauliflower 28
    Cauliflower with Tofu 29

    Carrots with Green Beans 30

    Bell Peppers with Potatoes 31

    Mushrooms with Peas 32

    Sweet Potato with Broccoli 33

    Seasoned Veggies 33

    Glazed Veggies 34

    Parmesan Veggies 35

    Potato Gratin 36

    Stuffed Eggplant 37

    Stuffed Bell Peppers 38

    Veggies Loaf 39

    Veggie Rice 40

    Potatoes 41

Snacks & Appetizers 42

    Polenta Sticks 42

    Pickle Slices 43

    Spicy Onion Rings 44

    Avocado Fries 45

    French Fries 46

    Jalapeño Poppers 47

    Cauliflower Poppers 48

    Broccoli Bites 49

    Chicken Nuggets 50

    Salmon Croquettes 51

    Beef Taquitos 52

Fish and Seafood Recipes 53

    Crispy Tilapia 53

    Simple Haddock 54

    Crispy Haddock 55

    Vinegar Halibut 56

    Breaded Cod 57

    Spicy Catfish 58

    Tuna Burgers 59

    Crab Cakes 60

    Crispy Prawns 61

    Prawns in Butter Sauce 61

    Lemony Shrimp 62

    Breaded Shrimp 63

    Coconut Shrimp 64

    Bacon-Wrapped Shrimp 65

Poultry Recipes 66

    BBQ Chicken Wings 66

    Buffalo Chicken Wings 67

    Parmesan Chicken Tenders 68

    Seasoned Chicken Tenders 69

    Chicken Cordon Bleu 70

    Simple Turkey Breast 71

    Herbed Turkey Breast 72

    Spiced Turkey Breast 73

    Herbed Duck Breast 74

    Garlicky Duck Legs 75

    Chicken with Avocado & Radish Bowl 75

    Savory Chicken with Onion 76

    Savory Buffalo Chicken 76

    Basil Cheese Chicken 77

Meat Recipes 78

    Bacon Wrapped Filet Mignon 78

    Beef Jerky 79

    Meatballs 80

    Beef Burgers 81

    Beef Casserole 82

    Garlicky Pork Tenderloin 82

    Glazed Pork Tenderloin 83

    Buttered Pork Loin 84

    Spicy Pork Shoulder 85

    BBQ Pork Ribs 86

    Seasoned Pork Chops 87

    Glazed Ham 88

    Crusted Rack of Lamb 89

    Lemony Lamb Chops 90

    Herbed Lamb Chops 91

    Beef Burgers with Parsley & Oregano 92

    Beef with Cauliflower and Green Peas 93

    Awesome Rib Eye Steak 93

Desserts Recipes **94**
   Apple Pie Rolls 94
   Berry Tacos 95
   Cinnamon Donuts 96
   Chocolate Cupcakes 97
   Banana Mug Cake 98
   Rum Cake 99
   Cherry Clafoutis 100
   Blueberry Cobbler 101
   Apple Crumble 102
   Strawberry Cheesecake 103
   Vanilla Lemon Cheesecake 104

INTRODUCTION

The Instant Vortex Air Fryer Oven swirls a breath of fresh air into your kitchen. Enjoy all the flavor of deep fried, all the benefits of air fried, and all the reliability and convenience of an Instant multifunctional appliance. With one appliance, you can Air Fry, Roast, Bake, Broil, Reheat, Dehydrate and Rotisserie cook your food.

Air frying replaces hot oil with super-heated circulating air to produce the same crunchy browned taste and texture that makes deep fried food so good. It still traps juicy moisture inside the crispy coating, but it does so without all the things that make people avoid deep frying: it's quicker, cleaner, healthier, and a whole lot easier.

Air fryers are also far more versatile than a deep fryer, which can only do one thing. In addition to cooking fried foods like french fries, fritters, and falafels, air frying also lets you grill a steak, roast a chicken or vegetables, bake a pizza or potatoes or meatloaf, dehydrate fruit, or crisp up some veggie chips. Love doughnuts? You can make those too. Chicken wings? Amazing! And if your food is frozen, that's okay. You don't need to thaw it first. Nuggets never tasted better, straight from the freezer.

COOKING WITH INSTANT VORTEX AIR FRYER OVEN

Smart and reliable
Made by the same people who brought you the Instant Pot, with all the same sort of smart programming

Versatile and convenient
Go beyond a single cooking style, use its large 10 quart capacity for all 7 built-in Smart Programs: Air Fry, Roast, Broil, Bake, Reheat, Dehydrate, plus with an option to Rotate for rotisserie-style cooking

One-Step Even Crisp Technology
Use the rotisserie basket to make crispy potato and sweet potato fries from fresh or frozen, toast nuts, roast vegetables, and make perfect chicken wings from fresh or frozen

Crisp but juicy
Savor the robust taste and crunchy browned texture of deep fried with just a few drops of oil

Quick and clean
Cook faster than deep frying, but with less mess and less waste

Healthy and responsible
Save electricity while you lock in all your food's natural nutrients without adding unwanted grease or fats

COOKING TIMETABLE

Food	Setting	Cook Time*	Temperature*	Accessory & Placement
Thin-cut fries (Frozen)	Air Fry/Roast	14-18 minutes	400°F	Rotisserie Basket
Thin-cut fries (Fresh)	Air Fry/Roast	18-20 minutes	400°F	Rotisserie Basket
Thick-cut fries (Frozen)	Air Fry/Roast	16-20 minutes	400°F	Rotisserie Basket
Thick-cut fries (Fresh)	Air Fry/Roast	20-25 minutes	400°F	Rotisserie Basket
Chicken wings (Fresh)	Air Fry/Roast	20-30 minutes	360°F	Cooking Tray, Bottom / Rotisserie Basket
Shrimp (Frozen)	Air Fry	8 minutes	400°F	Cooking Tray, Middle / Rotisserie Basket
Salmon (Fresh)	Broil	10 minutes	400°F	Cooking Tray, Middle
Shrimp (Fresh)	Air Fry	8-10 minutes	350°F	Cooking Tray, Middle / Rotisserie Basket
Asparagus	Broil/Bake	7-9 minutes	370°F	Cooking Tray, Middle / Rotisserie Basket
Sweet Corn	Roast	10 minutes	400°F	Cooking Tray, Middle
Cauliflower	Broil/Bake	6-10 minutes	370°F	Cooking Tray, Middle / Rotisserie Basket
Cauliflower Bites	Air Fry	15 minutes	380°F	Rotisserie Basket
Falafel	Air Fry	17 minutes	380°F	Rotisserie Basket
Whole chicken (up to 4 lbs.)	Roast	30-40 minutes	380°F	Rotisserie Spit
Chicken (Skewer)	Roast	30-40 minutes	380°F	Rotisserie Basket
Chicken nuggets (Frozen)	Broil	12-15 minutes	400°F	Cooking Tray, Middle
Souvlaki (Skewer)	Roast	16 minutes	380°F	Cooking Tray, Middle
Beef Jerky	Dehydrate	5 hours	135°F	Drip Pan, Bottom (Springform Pan)
Fish sticks (Frozen)	Broil	8-12 minutes	400°F	Cooking Tray, Middle
Nachos	Broil	2 minutes	400°F	Cooking Tray, Middle
Pizza (Fresh)	Bake	20 minutes	400°F	Cooking Tray, Middle
Spanakopita	Bake	10 minutes	330°F	Cooking Tray, Middle
Muffin	Bake	20 minutes	330°F	Cooking Tray, Middle
Cake	Bake	25-35 minutes	360°F	Drip Pan, Bottom (Springform Pan)
Fruit (Kiwi)	Dehydrate	6 hours	135°F	Drip Pan, Bottom (Springform Pan)

FAQ: INSTANT VORTEX AIR FRYER OVEN & FOOD

HOW DO AIR FRYERS OVENS WORK?

Air fryer ovens operate in 3 distinct ways:

As a convection oven with a low fan speed for most baking needs
As an air fryer with a powerful fan speed to quickly brown and give food a distinctive crispy, deep-fried flavor and texture
As a rotisserie oven with One-Step Even Crisp™ technology—put your food in and let the Vortex Plus do the rest
The Vortex Plus reaches a maximum temperature of 205°C / 400°F.

IS AIR FRYING A HEALTHIER FOOD PREPARATION OPTION THAN DEEP FRYING?

Yes! Air frying is a healthier choice in food preparation. Instead of submerging food in oil or fat, simply toss your food in a small amount of oil (as little as 2 tablespoons) to create beautiful, crispy golden french fries, chicken wings, fish and zucchini sticks, mushroom caps, and much more.

WHAT FOODS WORK BEST IN THE VORTEX PLUS?

You can make all kinds of things in the air fryer oven!

All your favorite fried and pan-fried dishes, like sausage, schnitzel and steak
Yummy baked dishes like pizzas, pies and cakes
Fresh or frozen convenience foods like fries, wings and mozza sticks are a snap
Cool healthy snacks like kale, beet, and sweet potato chips, or homemade fruit leather roll-ups
Do-it-yourself dehydrated jerky with beef, buffalo, trout, turkey, venison, elk, kangaroo, wild boar and so much more!
Compared to a full-sized oven, the Vortex Plus is also a fast, convenient and energy-efficient way to reheat and re-crisp leftovers.

CAN I USE MY VORTEX PLUS TO CRISP UP FROZEN FRIES AND FISH STICKS, OR PRE-DEEP-FRIED CHICKEN WINGS OR FINGERS?

Yes! The Vortex Plus is an easy way to add crispness to your favorite convenient foods.

Using the rotisserie feature makes getting the perfect all-over crunch even easier, with One-Step Even Crisp™ technology.

ARE THERE FOODS THAT CANNOT BE COOKED IN MY VORTEX PLUS AIR FRYER OVEN?

Anything you can cook in a conventional oven can be cooked in your Vortex Plus, but for best results, always space out foods so air has room to circulate freely, and cook in small batches.

Avoid foods dipped in batter, such as calamari, tempura shrimp and buttermilk fried chicken. If you want breading, go for an egg wash and breadcrumb coating.

HOW MUCH FOOD CAN I FIT IN MY VORTEX PLUS?

You can fit a lot in the air fryer oven, but for best results, remember to give your food room to breathe and don't crowd food items.

Place food items in a single layer or use the multi-level air fryer basket, and ensure there is room for the hot air to circulate freely.

DO I NEED TO PREHEAT THE VORTEX PLUS?

We recommend preheating the Vortex Plus as most food items benefit greatly from the immediate high heat of a preheated cooking chamber — preheating only takes 5 minutes!

Unless otherwise specified in a trusted recipe, the only time you should not preheat your air fryer oven is when using the rotisserie setting. Always properly install your food and rotisserie accessories into the oven's cooking chamber before turning the oven on.

WHAT HAPPENS IF DON'T TURN MY FOOD WHEN REMINDED TO?

Depending on the Smart Program, the Vortex Plus may beep part way through to remind you to turn your food. If you don't open the oven door, the air fryer continues cooking at the selected temperature until the timer completes.
Depending on the food item, failing to turn your food may result in uneven cooking. Refer to the Troubleshooting table in the User Manual for further assistance.

WHAT CAN I BAKE IN THE VORTEX PLUS AIR FRYER OVEN? DO I NEED A SPECIAL BAKING DISH?

Anything you can bake in an oven, you can bake in your Vortex Plus air fryer oven!
Use the provided multi-level air fryer basket to bake with, or any oven-safe baking dish, as long as it fits in the air fryer and leaves room for air to circulate freely.

MY FOOD IS NOT CRISPY-WHAT AM I DOING WRONG?

Your Vortex Plus air fryer oven is designed to produce deep-fried results without being submerged in oil, but it may need help from you:
Pat dry moist food items (like potato or zucchini sticks) with a clean dish towel or paper towel
Toss your food in up to 2 tablespoons of oil
Preheat the air fryer to blast your food with hot air
Turn or toss your food in the basket when reminded, or,
Use the rotisserie setting for One-Step Even Crisp™ technology—the Vortex Plus turns your food for you and produces a beautiful all-over crunch
Always follow a trusted recipe when air frying.

I HAVE BIRDS, IS THE VORTEX PLUS SAFE TO USE AROUND THEM?

No, some accessories may be coated with a non-stick coating that is not safe for use around birds and small pets.

BREAKFAST AND BRUNCH RECIPES

EGGS IN BREAD CUPS

Cooking Time: 12 minutes | Serves: 2

Ingredients:
- Butter – ½ tsp.
- Bread slices – 2
- Pancetta slice – 1, chopped
- Tomato slices – 4
- Mozzarella cheese – 1 tbsp. shredded
- Eggs – 2
- Maple syrup – 1/8 tsp.
- Balsamic vinegar – 1/8 tsp.
- Fresh parsley – ¼ tsp. chopped
- Salt and ground black pepper, as required

Directions:

Grease 2 ramekins. Line each prepared ramekin with 1 bread slice. Divide bacon and tomato slices over bread slice evenly in each ramekin. Top with the cheese evenly. Crack 1 egg in each ramekin over cheese. Drizzle with maple syrup and balsamic vinegar and then sprinkle with parsley, salt and black pepper. Arrange the ramekins on top of a cooking rack. Arrange the drip pan in the bottom of Instant Vortex Air Fryer Oven cooking chamber. Select "Air Fry" and then adjust the temperature to 320 °F. Set the time for 12 minutes and press "Start". When the display shows "Add Food" insert the cooking rack in the center position. When the display shows "Turn Food" do not turn food. When cooking time is complete, remove the ramekins from Vortex Oven. Serve warm.

EGGS IN AVOCADO CUPS

Cooking Time: 10 minutes | Serves: 2

Ingredients:
- Avocado – 1, halved and pitted
- Large eggs – 2
- Salt and ground black pepper, as required
- Cooked bacon slices – 2, crumbled

Directions:
Carefully, scoop out about 2 tsp. of flesh from each avocado half. Crack 1 egg in each avocado half and sprinkle with salt and black pepper. Arrange the avocado halves onto the lightly greased cooking tray. Arrange the drip pan in the bottom of Instant Vortex Air Fryer Oven cooking chamber. Select "Roast" and then adjust the temperature to 375 °F. Set the time for 10 minutes and press "Start". When the display shows "Add Food" insert the cooking tray in the center position. When the display shows "Turn Food" do not turn food. When cooking time is complete, remove the tray from Vortex Oven. Top each avocado half with bacon pieces and serve.

SAUSAGE WITH EGGS

Cooking Time: 6 minutes | Serves: 2

Ingredients:
- Breakfast sausages – 4
- Hard-boiled eggs – 2, peeled
- Avocado – 1, peeled, pitted and sliced

Directions:
Arrange the sausages in the rotisserie basket and attach the lid. Arrange the drip pan in the bottom of Instant Vortex Air Fryer Oven cooking chamber. Select "Roast" and then adjust the temperature to 375 °F. Set the time for 6 minutes and press "Start". When the display shows "Add Food" arrange the rotisserie basket, on the rotisserie spit. Then, close the door and touch "Rotate". When cooking time is complete, press the red lever to release the rod. Remove from the Vortex and place the sausages onto serving plates. Divide eggs and avocado slices onto each plate and serve.

CHICKEN OMELET

Cooking Time: 16 minutes | Serves: 2

Ingredients:
- Butter – 1 tsp.
- Small yellow onion – 1, chopped
- Jalapeño pepper – ½, seeded and chopped
- Eggs – 3
- Salt and ground black pepper, as required
- Cooked chicken – ¼ cup, shredded

Directions:

In a frying pan, melt the butter over medium heat and cook the onion for about 4-5 minutes. Add the jalapeño pepper and cook for about 1 minute. Remove from the heat and set aside to cool slightly. Meanwhile, in a bowl, add the eggs, salt, and black pepper and beat well. Add the onion mixture and chicken and stir to combine. Place the chicken mixture into a baking dish that will fit in the Vortex Air Fryer Oven. Arrange the drip pan in the bottom of Instant Vortex Air Fryer Oven cooking chamber. Select "Air Fry" and then adjust the temperature to 355 °F. Set the time for 6 minutes and press "Start". When the display shows "Add Food" insert the baking dish in the center position. When the display shows "Turn Food" do not turn food. When cooking time is complete, remove the baking dish from Vortex Oven. Cut the omelet into 2 portions and serve hot.

BACON & SAUSAGE OMELET

Cooking Time: 10 minutes | Serves: 2

Ingredients:
- Eggs – 4
- Ground black pepper, as required
- Bacon slice – 1, chopped
- Sausages – 2, chopped
- Onion – 1, chopped
- Fresh parsley – 1 tsp. minced

Directions:

In a bowl, crack the eggs and black pepper and beat well. Add the remaining ingredients and gently, stir to combine. Place the mixture into a baking dish that will fit in the Vortex Air Fryer Oven. Arrange the drip pan in the bottom of the Instant Vortex Air Fryer Oven cooking chamber. Select "Air Fry" and then adjust the temperature to 320 °F. Set the time for 10 minutes and press "Start". When the display shows "Add Food" place the baking dish over the drip pan. When the display shows "Turn Food" do not turn food. When cooking time is complete, remove the pan from Vortex Oven. Serve warm.

ZUCCHINI OMELET

Cooking Time: 14 minutes | Serves: 2

Ingredients:
- Butter – 1 tsp.
- Zucchini – 1, julienned
- Eggs – 4
- Fresh basil – ¼ tsp., chopped
- Red pepper flakes – ¼ tsp. crushed
- Salt and ground black pepper, as required

Directions:
In a skillet, melt the butter over medium heat and cook the zucchini for about 3-4 minutes. Remove the skillet from heat and set aside to cool slightly. Meanwhile, in a bowl, mix together the eggs, basil, red pepper flakes, salt, and black pepper. Add the cooked zucchini and gently, stir to combine. Place the zucchini mixture into a baking dish that will fit in the Vortex Air Fryer Oven. Arrange the drip pan in the bottom of Instant Vortex Air Fryer Oven cooking chamber. Select "Air Fry" and then adjust the temperature to 355 °F. Set the time for 10 minutes and press "Start". When the display shows "Add Food" insert the baking dish in the center position. When the display shows "Turn Food" do not turn food. When cooking time is complete, remove the baking dish from the Vortex Oven. Cut the omelet into 2 portions and serve hot.

BACON & SPINACH QUICHE

Cooking Time: 10 minutes | Serves: 4

Ingredients:
- Cooked bacon slices – 2, chopped
- Fresh spinach – ½ cup, chopped
- Mozzarella cheese – ¼ cup, shredded
- Parmesan cheese – ½ cup, shredded
- Milk – 2 tbsp.
- Tabasco sauce – 2 dashes
- Salt and ground black pepper, as required

Directions:
Add all the ingredients into a bowl and mix well. Transfer the mixture into a lightly greased baking dish that will fit in the Vortex Air Fryer Oven. Arrange the drip pan in the bottom of Instant Vortex Air Fryer Oven cooking chamber. Select "Air Fry" and then adjust the temperature to 320 °F. Set the time for 10 minutes and press "Start". When the display shows "Add Food" place the baking dish over the drip pan. When the display shows "Turn Food" do not turn food. When cooking time is complete, remove the baking dish from Vortex Oven. Cut into equal-sized wedges and serve hot.

MACARONI QUICHES

Cooking Time: 20 minutes | Serves: 4

Ingredients:
- Shortcrust pastry – 1
- Leftover macaroni n' cheese – ½ cup
- Plain Greek yogurt – 2 tbsps.
- Garlic puree – 1 tsp.
- Milk – 11 oz.
- Large eggs – 2
- Parmesan cheese – 2 tbsps. grated

Directions:

Dust 4 ramekins with a little flour. Line the bottom of each prepared ramekin with shortcrust pastry. In a bowl, mix together macaroni, yogurt and garlic. Place the macaroni mixture into the prepared ramekins about ¾ full. In a small bowl, add the milk and eggs and beat well. Place the egg mixture over the macaroni mixture and top with the cheese evenly. Arrange the ramekins on top of a cooking rack. Arrange the drip pan in the bottom of Instant Vortex Air Fryer Oven cooking chamber. Select "Air Fry" and then adjust the temperature to 355 °F. Set the time for 20 minutes and press "Start". When the display shows "Add Food" insert the cooking rack in the center position. When the display shows "Turn Food" do not turn food. When cooking time is complete, remove the ramekins from the Vortex Oven. Serve hot.

TROUT FRITTATA

Cooking Time: 25 minutes | Serves: 4

Ingredients:
- Olive oil – 1 tbsp.
- Onion – 1, sliced
- Eggs – 6
- Horseradish sauce – ½ tbsp.
- Crème Fraiche – 2 tbsps.
- Hot-smoked trout fillets – 2, chopped
- Fresh dill – ¼ cup, chopped

Directions:

In a skillet, heat the oil over medium heat and cook the onion for about 4-5 minutes. Remove from the heat and set aside. Meanwhile, in a bowl, add the eggs, horseradish sauce, and crème fraiche and mix well. Place the cooked onion into a baking dish that will fit in the Vortex Air Fryer Oven. Arrange the drip pan in the bottom of the Instant Vortex Air Fryer Oven cooking chamber. Top the onion with the egg mixture, followed by trout. Select "Air Fry" and then adjust the temperature to 320 °F. Set the time for 20 minutes and press "Start". When the display shows "Add Food" insert the baking dish in the center position. When the display shows "Turn Food" do not turn food. When cooking time is complete, remove the baking dish from Vortex Oven. Cut into equal-sized wedges and serve with the garnishing of dill.

MIXED VEGGIE FRITTATA

Cooking Time: 15 minutes | Serves: 4

Ingredients:
- Eggs – 4
- Heavy cream – 3 tbsps.
- Salt, as required
- Cheddar cheese – 4 tbsps. grated
- Fresh mushrooms – 4, sliced
- Fresh spinach – 4 tbsps. chopped
- Grape tomatoes – 3, halved
- Fresh mixed herbs – 2 tbsps. chopped
- Scallion – 1, sliced

Directions:

In a bowl, add the eggs, cream and salt and beat well. Add the remaining ingredients and stir to combine. Place the mixture into a greased baking dish that will fit in the Vortex Air Fryer Oven. Arrange the drip pan in the bottom of the Instant Vortex Air Fryer Oven cooking chamber. Select "Air Fry" and then adjust the temperature to 350 °F. Set the time for 15 minutes and press "Start". When the display shows "Add Food" place the baking dish over the drip pan. When the display shows "Turn Food" do not turn food. When cooking time is complete, remove the baking dish from the Vortex Oven. Serve warm.

TURKEY & SPINACH CUPS

Cooking Time: 23 minutes | Serves: 2

Ingredients:

- Unsalted butter – 1 tbsp.
- Fresh baby spinach – 1 lb.
- Eggs – 4
- Cooked turkey – 7 oz. chopped
- Milk – 4 tsps.
- Salt and ground black pepper, as required

Directions:

In a skillet, melt the butter over medium heat and cook the spinach for about 2-3 minutes or until just wilted. Remove from the heat and transfer the spinach into a bowl. Set aside to cool slightly. Divide the spinach into 4 greased ramekins, followed by the turkey. Crack 1 egg into each ramekin and drizzle with milk. Sprinkle with salt and black pepper. Arrange the ramekins on top of a cooking rack. Arrange the drip pan in the bottom of Instant Vortex Air Fryer Oven cooking chamber. Select "Air Fry" and then adjust the temperature to 355 °F. Set the time for 20 minutes and press "Start". When the display shows "Add Food" insert the cooking rack in the center position. When the display shows "Turn Food" do not turn food. When cooking time is complete, remove the ramekins from Vortex Oven. Serve warm.

SAVORY CARROT MUFFINS

Cooking Time: 7 minutes | Serves: 6

Ingredients:

For Muffins:
- Whole-wheat flour – ¼ cup
- All-purpose flour – ¼ cup
- Baking powder – ½ tsp.
- Baking soda – 1/8 tsp.
- Dried parsley – ½ tsp. crushed
- Salt – ½ tsp.
- Plain yogurt – ½ cup
- White vinegar – 1 tsp.
- Vegetable oil – 1 tbsp.
- Cottage cheese – 3 tbsps.
- Carrot – 1, peeled and grated
- Water – 2-4 tbsp. (if needed)

For Topping:
- Parmesan cheese – 7 oz. grated
- Walnuts – ¼ cup, chopped

Directions:

For muffin: in a large bowl, mix together the flours, baking powder, baking soda, parsley, and salt. In another large bowl, mix well the yogurt, and vinegar. Add the remaining ingredients except water and beat them well. (Add some water if needed). With your hands, make a well in center of the yogurt mixture. Slowly, add the flour mixture in the well and mix until thoroughly combined. Place the mixture into 6 lightly greased muffin molds evenly and top with the Parmesan cheese and walnuts. Arrange the muffin molds on top of a cooking rack. Arrange the drip pan in the bottom of Instant Vortex Air Fryer Oven cooking chamber. Select "Air Fry" and then adjust the temperature to 355 °F. Set the time for 7 minutes and press "Start". When the display shows "Add Food" insert the cooking rack in the center position. When the display shows "Turn Food" do not turn food. When cooking time is complete, remove the muffin molds from Vortex Oven. Place the muffin molds onto a wire rack to cool for about 5 minutes. Carefully, invert the muffins onto the platter and serve warm.

SWEET POTATO ROSTI

Cooking Time: 15 minutes | Serves: 2

Ingredients:
- Sweet potatoes – ½ lb. peeled, grated and squeezed
- Fresh parsley – 1 tbsp. chopped finely
- Salt and ground black pepper, as required
- Sour cream – 2 tbsps.

Directions:
In a large bowl, mix together the grated sweet potato, parsley, salt, and black pepper. Arrange the drip pan in the bottom of Instant Vortex Air Fryer Oven cooking chamber. Select "Air Fry" and then adjust the temperature to 355 °F. Set the time for 15 minutes and press "Start". Arrange the sweet potato mixture onto the lightly greased cooking tray and shape it into an even circle. When the display shows "Add Food" insert the cooking tray in the center position. When the display shows "Turn Food" do not turn food. When cooking time is complete, remove the tray from Vortex Oven. Cut the sweet potato rosti into wedges. Top with the sour cream and serve immediately.

ZUCCHINI FRITTERS

Cooking Time: 7 minutes | Serves: 4

Ingredients:
- Zucchini – 10½ oz. grated and squeezed
- Halloumi cheese – 7 oz.
- All-purpose flour – ¼ cup
- Eggs – 2
- Fresh dill – 1 tsp. minced
- Salt and ground black pepper, as required

Directions:
In a large bowl mix together all the ingredients. Make small-sized fritters from the mixture. Arrange the drip pan in the bottom of Instant Vortex Air Fryer Oven cooking chamber. Select "Air Fry" and then adjust the temperature to 355 °F. Set the time for 7 minutes and press "Start". Arrange the fritters onto the lightly greased cooking tray. When the display shows "Add Food" insert the cooking tray in the center position. When the display shows "Turn Food" turn the fritters. When cooking time is complete, remove the tray from Vortex Oven. Serve warm.

OATS, NUTS & SEEDS GRANOLA

Cooking Time: 15 minutes | Serves: 8

Ingredients:
- Olive oil – 1/3 cup
- Maple syrup – ¼ cup
- Honey – 2 tbsps.
- Vanilla extract – ½ tsp.
- Rolled oats – 2 cups
- Wheat germ – ½ cup, toasted
- Dried cherries – ¼ cup
- Dried blueberries – ¼ cup
- Dried cranberries – 2 tbsps.
- Sunflower seeds – 2 tbsps.
- Pumpkin seeds – 2 tbsps. shelled
- Flaxseed – 1 tbsp.
- Pecans – 2 tbsps. chopped
- Hazelnuts – 2 tbsps. chopped
- Almonds – 2 tbsps. chopped
- Walnuts – 2 tbsps. chopped
- Ground cinnamon – ½ tsp.
- Ground cloves – 1/8 tsp.
- Ground nutmeg – 1/8 tsp.

Directions:

In a small bowl, add the oil and maple syrup and mix well. In a large bowl, add the remaining ingredients and mix well. Add the oil mixture and mix until well combined. Place the mixture into a baking dish that will fit in the Vortex Air Fryer Oven. Arrange the drip pan in the bottom of the Instant Vortex Air Fryer Oven cooking chamber. Select "Air Fry" and then adjust the temperature to 350 °F. Set the time for 15 minutes and press "Start". When the display shows "Add Food" insert the baking dish in the center position. Stir the granola after every 5 minutes. When cooking time is complete, remove the baking dish from the Vortex Oven. Set the granola aside to cool completely before serving.

VEGETARIAN RECIPES

BUFFALO CAULIFLOWER

Cooking Time: 12 minutes | Serves: 4

Ingredients:
- Large head cauliflower – 1, cut into bite-size florets
- Olive oil – 1 tbsp.
- Garlic powder – 2 tsps.
- Salt and ground black pepper, as required
- Butter – 1 tbsp. melted
- Warm buffalo sauce – 2/3 cup

Directions:

In a large bowl, add cauliflower florets, oil, garlic powder, salt and black pepper and toss to coat. Arrange the cauliflower florets onto the greased cooking tray in a single layer. Arrange the drip pan in the bottom of the Instant Vortex Air Fryer Oven cooking chamber. Select "Air Fry" and then adjust the temperature to 375 °F. Set the time for 12 minutes and press "Start". When the display shows "Add Food" insert the cooking tray in the center position. When the display shows "Turn Food" coat the cauliflower florets with buffalo sauce. When cooking time is complete, remove the tray from Vortex Oven. Serve hot.

CAULIFLOWER WITH TOFU

Cooking Time: 15 minutes | Serves: 2

Ingredients:
- Firm tofu – 7-oz. pressed and cubed
- Small head cauliflower – ½, cut into florets
- Canola oil – 1 tbsp.
- Nutritional yeast – 1 tbsp.
- Dried parsley – ¼ tsp.
- Ground turmeric – 1 tsp.
- Paprika – ¼ tsp.
- Salt and ground black pepper, as required

Directions:

In a bowl, mix together the tofu, cauliflower and the remaining ingredients. Place the tofu mixture in the greased cooking tray. Arrange the drip pan in the bottom of the Instant Vortex Air Fryer Oven cooking chamber. Select "Air Fry" and then adjust the temperature to 390 °F. Set the time for 15 minutes and press "Start". When the display shows "Add Food" insert the cooking tray in the center position. When the display shows "Turn Food" turn the tofu mixture. When cooking time is complete, remove the tray from the Vortex Oven. Serve hot.

CARROTS WITH GREEN BEANS

Cooking Time: 10 minutes | Serves: 3

Ingredients:
- Green beans – ½ lb. trimmed
- Carrots – ½ lb. peeled and cut into sticks
- Olive oil – 1 tbsp.
- Salt and ground black pepper, as required

Directions:

Add all the ingredients into a bowl and toss to coat well. Place the vegetables in the rotisserie basket and attach the lid. Arrange the drip pan in the bottom of the Instant Vortex Air Fryer Oven cooking chamber. Select "Air Fry" and then adjust the temperature to 400 °F. Set the time for 10 minutes and press "Start". Then, close the door and touch "Rotate". When the display shows "Add Food" arrange the rotisserie basket, on the rotisserie spit. Then, close the door and touch "Rotate". When cooking time is complete, press the red lever to release the rod. Remove from the Vortex Oven. Serve hot.

BELL PEPPERS WITH POTATOES

Cooking Time: 6 minutes | Serves: 2

Ingredients:
- Water – 2 cups
- Russet potatoes – 5, peeled and cubed
- Extra-virgin olive oil – ½ tbsp.
- Onion – ½, chopped
- Jalapeño pepper – ½, chopped
- Large bell pepper – 1, seeded and chopped
- Dried oregano – ¼ tsp. crushed
- Garlic powder – ¼ tsp.
- Ground cumin – ¼ tsp.
- Red chili powder – ¼ tsp.
- Salt and ground black pepper, as required

Directions:

In a large bowl, add the water and potatoes and set aside for about 30 minutes. Drain well and pat dry with the paper towels. In a bowl, add the potatoes and oil and toss to coat well. Arrange the potato cubes onto the greased rack. Arrange the drip pan in the bottom of Instant Vortex Air Fryer Oven cooking chamber. Select "Air Fry" and then adjust the temperature to 330 °F. Set the time for 5 minutes and press "Start". When the display shows "Add Food" insert the cooking rack in the center position. When the display shows "Turn Food" do not turn food. When cooking time is complete, remove the tray from the Vortex Oven. Transfer the potato cubes into a large bowl with remaining ingredients and toss to coat well. Place the veggie mixture onto the greased cooking pan and spread in an even layer. Select "Air Fry" and then adjust the temperature to 390 °F. Set the time for 20 minutes and press "Start". When the display shows "Add Food" insert the cooking rack in the center position. When the display shows "Turn Food" turn the vegetables. When cooking time is complete, remove the tray from the Vortex Oven. Serve hot.

MUSHROOMS WITH PEAS

Cooking Time: 16 minutes | Serves: 4

Ingredients:
- Soy sauce – ½ cup
- Maple syrup – 4 tbsps.
- Rice vinegar – 4 tbsps.
- Garlic cloves – 4, chopped finely
- Chinese five-spice powder – 2 tsps.
- Ground ginger – ½ tsp.
- Cremini mushrooms – 16 oz., halved
- Frozen peas – ½ cup

Directions:

Grease a baking dish that will fit in the Vortex Air Fryer Oven. In a bowl, add the soy sauce, maple syrup, vinegar, garlic, five-spice powder, and ground ginger and mix well. Set aside. Place the mushroom into the prepared baking dish in a single layer. Arrange the drip pan in the bottom of the Instant Vortex Air Fryer Oven cooking chamber. Select "Air Fry" and then adjust the temperature to 350 °F. Set the time for 15 minutes and press "Start". When the display shows "Add Food" insert the baking dish in the center position. When the display shows "Turn Food" add the peas and vinegar mixture into the baking dish and stir to combine. When cooking time is complete, remove the baking dish from the Vortex Oven. Serve hot.

SWEET POTATO WITH BROCCOLI

Cooking Time: 20 minutes | Serves: 4

Ingredients:
- Medium sweet potatoes – 2, peeled and cut in 1-inch cubes
- Broccoli head – 1, cut in 1-inch florets
- Vegetable oil – 2 tbsps.
- Salt and ground black pepper, as required

Directions:
Grease a baking dish that will fit in the Vortex Air Fryer Oven. Add all the ingredients into a bowl and toss to coat well. Place the veggie mixture into the prepared baking dish in a single layer. Arrange the drip pan in the bottom of Instant Vortex Air Fryer Oven cooking chamber. Select "Roast" and then adjust the temperature to 415 °F. Set the time for 20 minutes and press "Start". When the display shows "Add Food" insert the baking dish in the center position. When the display shows "Turn Food" turn the vegetables. When cooking time is complete, remove the baking dish from the Vortex Oven. Serve hot.

SEASONED VEGGIES

Cooking Time: 12 minutes | Serves: 4

Ingredients:
- Baby carrots – 1 cup
- Broccoli florets – 1 cup
- Cauliflower florets – 1 cup
- Olive oil – 1 tbsp.
- Italian seasoning – 1 tbsp.
- Salt and ground black pepper, as required

Directions:
Add all the ingredients into a bowl and toss to coat well. Place the vegetables in the rotisserie basket and attach the lid. Arrange the drip pan in the bottom of the Instant Vortex Air Fryer Oven cooking chamber. Select "Air Fry" and then adjust the temperature to 380 °F. Set the time for 18 minutes and press "Start". Then, close the door and touch "Rotate". When the display shows "Add Food" arrange the rotisserie basket, on the rotisserie spit. Then, close the door and touch "Rotate". When cooking time is complete, press the red lever to release the rod. Remove from the Vortex Oven. Serve.

GLAZED VEGGIES

Cooking Time: 20 minutes | Serves: 4

Ingredients:
- Cherry tomatoes – 2 oz.
- Large parsnip – 1, peeled and chopped
- Large carrot – 1, peeled and chopped
- Large zucchini – 1, chopped
- Green bell pepper – 1, seeded and chopped
- Olive oil – 6 tbsps. divided
- Honey – 3 tbsps.
- Dijon mustard – 1 tsp.
- Mixed dried herbs – 1 tsp.
- Garlic paste – 1 tsp.
- Salt and ground black pepper, as required

Directions:

Grease a baking dish that will fit in the Vortex Air Fryer Oven. Place the vegetables into prepared baking dish and drizzle with 3 tbsps. of oil. Arrange the drip pan in the bottom of the Instant Vortex Air Fryer Oven cooking chamber. Select "Air Fry" and then adjust the temperature to 350 °F. Set the time for 15 minutes and press "Start". When the display shows "Add Food" insert the baking dish in the center position. Meanwhile, in a bowl, add the remaining oil, honey, mustard, herbs, garlic, salt, and black pepper and mix well. When the display shows "Turn Food" turn the veggies. When cooking time is complete, remove the baking dish from Vortex Oven. In the baking dish, add the honey mixture and mix until well combined. Again, select "Air Fry" and then adjust the temperature to 392 °F. Set the time for 5 minutes and press "Start". When the display shows "Add Food" insert the baking dish in the center position. When the display shows "Turn Food" turn the veggies. When cooking time is complete, remove the baking dish from Vortex Oven. Serve hot.

PARMESAN VEGGIES

Cooking Time: 19 minutes | Serves: 5

Ingredients:
- Olive oil – 1 tbsp.
- Garlic – 1 tbsp. minced
- Cauliflower florets – 1 cup
- Broccoli florets – 1 cup
- Zucchini – 1 cup, sliced
- Yellow squash – ½ cup, sliced
- Fresh mushrooms – ½ cup, sliced
- Small onion – 1, sliced
- Balsamic vinegar – ¼ cup
- Red pepper flakes – 1 tsp.
- Salt and ground black pepper, as required
- Parmesan cheese – ¼ cup, grated

Directions:
Add all the ingredients into a bowl except cheese and toss to coat well. Place the veggie mixture in the greased cooking tray. Arrange the drip pan in the bottom of the Instant Vortex Air Fryer Oven cooking chamber. Select "Air Fry" and then adjust the temperature to 390 °F. Set the time for 18 minutes and press "Start". When the display shows "Add Food" insert the cooking tray in the center position. When the display shows "Turn Food" turn the veggie mixture. After 16 minutes of cooking, sprinkle the vegetables with cheese evenly. When cooking time is complete, remove the tray from the Vortex Oven. Serve hot.

POTATO GRATIN

Cooking Time: 20 minutes | Serves: 4

Ingredients:

- Large potatoes – 2, sliced thinly
- Cream – 5½ tbsps.
- Eggs – 2
- Plain flour – 1 tbsp.
- Cheddar cheese – ½ cup, grated

Directions:

Arrange the potato cubes onto the greased rack. Arrange the drip pan in the bottom of the Instant Vortex Air Fryer Oven cooking chamber. Select "Air Fry" and then adjust the temperature to 355 °F. Set the time for 10 minutes and press "Start". When the display shows "Add Food" insert the cooking rack in the center position. When the display shows "Turn Food" do not turn food. Meanwhile, in a bowl, add cream, eggs and flour and mix until a thick sauce forms. When cooking time is complete, remove the tray from the Vortex Oven. Divide the potato slices into 4 lightly greased ramekins evenly and top with the egg mixture, followed by the cheese. Arrange the ramekins on top of a cooking rack. Again, select "Air Fry" and then adjust the temperature to 390 °F. Set the time for 10 minutes and press "Start". When the display shows "Add Food" insert the cooking rack in the center position. When the display shows "Turn Food" do not turn food. When cooking time is complete, remove the ramekins from the Vortex Oven. Serve warm.

STUFFED EGGPLANT

Cooking Time: 6 minutes | Serves: 2

Ingredients:
- Small eggplants – 4, halved lengthwise
- Fresh lime juice – 1 tsp.
- Vegetable oil – 1 tsp.
- Small onion – 1, chopped
- Garlic – ¼ tsp. chopped
- Small tomato – ½, chopped
- Salt and ground black pepper, as required
- Cottage cheese – 1 tbsp.
- Green bell pepper – ¼, seeded and chopped
- Tomato paste – 1 tbsp.
- Fresh cilantro – 1 tbsp. chopped

Directions:

Carefully, cut a slice from one side of each eggplant lengthwise. With a small spoon, scoop out the flesh from each eggplant leaving a thick shell. Transfer the eggplant flesh into a bowl. Drizzle the eggplants with lime juice evenly. Arrange the eggplants on top of the greased cooking rack. Arrange the drip pan in the bottom of the Instant Vortex Air Fryer Oven cooking chamber. Select "Air Fry" and then adjust the temperature to 320 °F. Set the timer for 3 minutes and press "Start". When the display shows "Add Food" insert the cooking rack in the center position. When the display shows "Turn Food" do not turn food. Meanwhile, in a skillet heat the oil over medium heat and sauté the onion and garlic for about 2 minutes. Add the eggplant flesh, tomato, salt, and black pepper and sauté for about 2 minutes. Stir in the cheese, bell pepper, tomato paste, and cilantro and cook for about 1 minute. Remove the pan of veggie mixture from heat. When cooking time is complete, remove the eggplants from the Vortex Oven. Arrange the cooked eggplants onto a plate and stuff each with the veggie mixture. Close each with its cut part. Arrange the eggplants on top of the greased cooking rack. Again, select "Air Fry" and then adjust the temperature to 355 °F. Set the time for 8 minutes and press "Start". When the display shows "Add Food" insert the cooking rack in the center position. When the display shows "Turn Food" do not turn food. When cooking time is complete, remove the eggplants from Vortex Oven. Serve hot.

STUFFED BELL PEPPERS

Cooking Time: 6 minutes | Serves: 3

Ingredients:

- Bell peppers – 6 large
- Bread roll – 1, chopped finely
- Carrot – 1, peeled and chopped finely
- Onion – 1, chopped finely
- Potato – 1, peeled and chopped finely
- Fresh peas – ½ cup, shelled
- Garlic cloves – 2, minced
- Fresh parsley – 2 tsp. chopped
- Salt and ground black pepper, as required
- Cheddar cheese – 1/3 cup, grated

Directions:

Remove the top of each bell pepper and discard the seeds. Finely chop the bell pepper tops. In a bowl, place bell pepper tops, bread loaf, vegetables, garlic, parsley, salt and black pepper and mix well. Stuff each bell pepper with the vegetable mixture. Arrange the bell peppers on top of the greased cooking rack. Arrange the drip pan in the bottom of Instant Vortex Air Fryer Oven cooking chamber. Select "Air Fry" and then adjust the temperature to 350 °F. Set the time for 25 minutes and press "Start". When the display shows "Add Food" insert the cooking rack in the center position. When the display shows "Turn Food" do not turn food. After 20 minutes, sprinkle each bell pepper with cheddar cheese. When cooking time is complete, remove the bell peppers from Vortex Oven. Serve hot.

VEGGIES LOAF

Cooking Time: 1½ hours | Serves: 6

Ingredients:

- Vegetable broth – 1 (14½-oz.) can
- Brown lentils – ¾ cup, rinsed
- Olive oil – 1 tbsp.
- Carrots – 1¾ cups, peeled and shredded
- Fresh mushrooms – 1 cup, chopped
- Onion – 1 cup, chopped
- Fresh parsley – 1 tbsp. minced
- Fresh basil – 1 tbsp. minced
- Cooked brown rice – ½ cup
- Mozzarella cheese – 1 cup, shredded
- Large egg – 1
- Large egg white – 1
- Salt and ground black pepper, as required
- Tomato paste – 2 tbsps.
- Water – 2 tbsps. water

Directions:

In a pan, place the broth over medium-high heat and bring to a boil. Stir in the lentils and again bring to a boil. Reduce the heat to low and simmer, covered for about 30 minutes. Remove from the heat and set aside to cool slightly. Meanwhile, in a large skillet, heat the oil over medium heat and sauté the carrots, mushrooms and onion for about 10 minutes. Stir in herbs and remove from the heat. Transfer the veggie mixture into a large bowl and set aside to cool slightly. After cooling, add the lentils, rice, cheese, egg, egg white and seasonings and lentils and mix until well combined. In a small bowl, stir together the tomato paste and water. Place the mixture into a greased parchment paper-lined loaf pan and top with water mixture. Arrange the drip pan in the bottom of the Instant Vortex Air Fryer Oven cooking chamber. Select "Bake" and then adjust the temperature to 350 °F. Set the time for 50 minutes and press "Start". When the display shows "Add Food" place the loaf pan over the drip pan. When the display shows "Turn Food" do not turn food. When cooking time is complete, remove the pan from the Vortex Oven and place the loaf pan onto a wire rack for about 10 minutes before slicing. Carefully, invert the loaf onto the wire rack. Cut into desired-sized slices and serve.

VEGGIE RICE

Cooking Time: 18 minutes | Serves: 4

Ingredients:

- Cooked white rice – 2 cups
- Vegetable oil – 1 tbsp.
- Sesame oil – 2 tsps. toasted and divided
- Water – 1 tbsp.
- Salt and ground white pepper, as required
- Large egg – 1, lightly beaten
- Frozen peas – ½ cup, thawed
- Frozen carrots – ½ cup, thawed
- Soy sauce – 1 tsp.
- Sriracha sauce – 1 tsp.
- Sesame seeds – ½ tsp. toasted
- Fresh parsley – 2 tbsps. chopped

Directions:

Grease a baking dish that will fit in the Vortex Air Fryer Oven. In a large bowl, add the rice, vegetable oil, one tsp. of sesame oil, water, salt and white pepper and mix well. Place the rice mixture into the prepared baking dish in an even layer. Arrange the drip pan in the bottom of the Instant Vortex Air Fryer Oven cooking chamber. Select "Air Fry" and then adjust the temperature to 380 °F. Set the time for 12 minutes and press "Start". When the display shows "Add Food" insert the baking dish in the center position. When the display shows "Turn Food" stir the rice mixture. When cooking time is complete, remove the baking dish from the Vortex Oven. Place the beaten egg over rice evenly. Select "Air Fry" and then adjust the temperature to 380 °F. Set the time for 2 minutes and press "Start". When the display shows "Add Food" insert the baking dish in the Hasselback

POTATOES

Cooking Time: 30 minutes | Serves: 4

Ingredients:
- 4 potatoes
- 2 tablespoons olive oil
- 2 tablespoons Parmesan cheese, shredded
- 1 tablespoon fresh chives, chopped

Directions:
1. With a sharp knife, cut slits along each potato the short way about ¼-inch apart, making sure slices should stay connected at the bottom.
2. Gently brush each potato evenly with oil
3. Press "Power Button" of Air Fry Oven and turn the dial to select the "Air Fry" mode.
4. Press the Time button and again turn the dial to set the cooking time to 30 minutes.
5. Now push the Temp button and rotate the dial to set the temperature at 355 degrees F.
6. Press "Start/Pause" button to start.
7. When the unit beeps to show that it is preheated, open the lid.
8. Arrange the potatoes in greased "Air Fry Basket" and insert in the oven.
9. Coat the potatoes with the oil once halfway through.
10. Transfer the potatoes onto a platter and top with the cheeses, and chives.
11. Serve immediately.

SNACKS & APPETIZERS

POLENTA STICKS

Cooking Time: 6 minutes | Serves: 4

Ingredients:
- Olive oil – 1 tbsp.
- Cooked polenta – 2½ cups
- Salt, as required
- Parmesan cheese – ¼ cup, shredded

Directions:

Place the polenta in a lightly greased baking dish that will fit in the Vortex Air Fryer Oven. With a plastic wrap, cover and refrigerate for about 1 hour or until set. Remove from the refrigerator and cut into desired-sized slices. Sprinkle with salt. Arrange the polenta sticks onto a greased cooking tray. Arrange the drip pan in the bottom of the Instant Vortex Air Fryer Oven cooking chamber. Select "Air Fry" and then adjust the temperature to 350 °F. Set the time for 6 minutes and press "Start". When the display shows "Add Food" insert the cooking tray in the center position. When the display shows "Turn Food" do not turn food. When cooking time is complete, remove the tray from the Vortex Oven. Top with cheese and serve.

PICKLE SLICES

Cooking Time: 18 minutes | Serves: 8

Ingredients:
- Dill pickle slices – 16
- All-purpose flour – ¼ cup
- Salt, as required
- Small eggs – 2, beaten lightly
- Dill pickle juice – 1 tbsp.
- Garlic powder – ¼ tsp.
- Cayenne pepper – ¼ tsp.
- Panko breadcrumbs – 1 cup
- Fresh dill – 1 tbsp. minced
- Cooking spray

Directions:
Place the pickle slices on paper towels for about 15 minutes or until all the liquid is absorbed. Meanwhile, in a shallow dish, add flour and salt and mix well. In another shallow dish, add the eggs, pickle juice, garlic powder and cayenne and beat until well combined. In a third shallow dish, add panko and dill and mix well. Coat the pickle slices with flour mixture, then dip into egg mixture and finally coat with the panko mixture. Spray the pickle slices with cooking spray. Arrange the pickle slices onto a cooking tray. Arrange the drip pan in the bottom of the Instant Vortex Air Fryer Oven cooking chamber. Select "Air Fry" and then adjust the temperature to 400 °F. Set the time for 18 minutes and press "Start". When the display shows "Add Food" insert the cooking tray in the center position. When the display shows "Turn Food" turn the pickle slices. When cooking time is complete, remove the tray from the Vortex Oven. Serve warm.

SPICY ONION RINGS

Cooking Time: 8 minutes | Serves: 4

Ingredients:
- Large onion – 1, cut into ½-inch thick rings
- Coconut flour – 3 tbsps.
- Salt, as required
- Large eggs – 2
- Pork rinds – 2/3 cup, crushed
- Blanched almond flour – 3 tbsps.
- Paprika – ½ tsp.
- Onion powder – ¼ tsp.
- Garlic powder – ¼ tsp.

Directions:

In a shallow dish, mix together the coconut flour and salt. In a second shallow dish, add the eggs and beat lightly. In a third shallow dish, add pork rinds, almond flour and spices and mix well. Coat the onion rings with flour mixture, then dip into egg whites and finally coat with the pork rind mixture. Arrange the coated onion rings onto 2 lightly greased cooking trays in a single layer. Arrange the drip pan in the bottom of Instant Vortex Air Fryer Oven cooking chamber. Select "Air Fry" and then adjust the temperature to 400 °F. Set the time for 8 minutes and press "Start". When the display shows "Add Food" insert 1 tray in the top position and another in the bottom position. When the display shows "Turn Food" do not turn the food but switch the position of cooking trays. When cooking time is complete, remove the trays from Vortex Oven. Serve hot.

AVOCADO FRIES

Cooking Time: 7 minutes | Serves: 2

Ingredients:
- All-purpose flour – ¼ cup
- Salt and ground black pepper, as required
- Egg – 1
- Water – 1 tsp.
- Panko breadcrumbs – ½ cup
- Avocado – 1, peeled, pitted and sliced into 8 pieces
- Nonstick cooking spray

Directions:

In a shallow bowl, mix together the flour, salt, and black pepper. In a second bowl, mix well egg and water. In a third bowl, put the breadcrumbs. Coat the avocado slices with flour mixture, then dip into egg mixture and finally, coat evenly with the breadcrumbs. Arrange the avocado slices onto the greased rack and spray with cooking spray. Arrange the drip pan in the bottom of the Instant Vortex Air Fryer Oven cooking chamber. Select "Air Fry" and then adjust the temperature to 400 °F. Set the timer for 7 minutes and press "Start". When the display shows "Add Food" insert the rack in the center position. When the display shows "Turn Food" do not turn food. When cooking time is complete, remove the rack from the Vortex Oven. Serve warm.

FRENCH FRIES

Cooking Time: 16 minutes | Serves: 2

Ingredients:

- Potatoes – ½ lb. peeled and cut into ½-inch thick sticks lengthwise
- Olive oil – 1 tbsp.
- Salt and ground black pepper, as required

Directions:

Add all the ingredients into a bowl and toss to coat well. Arrange the potato sticks onto a cooking tray. Arrange the drip pan in the bottom of the Instant Vortex Air Fryer Oven cooking chamber. Select "Air Fry" and then adjust the temperature to 400 °F. Set the time for 16 minutes and press "Start". When the display shows "Add Food" insert the cooking tray in the center position. When the display shows "Turn Food" turn the potato sticks. When cooking time is complete, remove the tray from the Vortex Oven. Serve warm.

JALAPEÑO POPPERS

Cooking Time: 13 minutes | Serves: 6

Ingredients:
- Large jalapeño peppers – 12
- Cream cheese – 8 oz. softened
- Scallion – ¼ cup, chopped
- Fresh cilantro – ¼ cup, chopped
- Onion powder – ¼ tsp.
- Garlic powder – ¼ tsp.
- Salt, as required
- Sharp Cheddar cheese – 1/3 cup, grated

Directions:
Carefully, cut off one-third of each pepper lengthwise and then, scoop out the seeds and membranes. In a bowl, mix together the cream cheese, scallion, cilantro, spices and salt. Stuff each pepper with the cream cheese mixture and top with Cheddar cheese. Arrange the jalapeño peppers onto a greased cooking tray. Arrange the drip pan in the bottom of the Instant Vortex Air Fryer Oven cooking chamber. Select "Air Fry" and then adjust the temperature to 400 °F. Set the time for 13 minutes and press "Start". When the display shows "Add Food" insert the cooking tray in the center position. When the display shows "Turn Food" do not turn food. When cooking time is complete, remove the tray from the Vortex Oven. Serve immediately.

CAULIFLOWER POPPERS

Cooking Time: 20 minutes | Serves: 6

Ingredients:
- Olive oil – 3 tbsps.
- Paprika – 1 tsp.
- Ground cumin – ½ tsp.
- Ground turmeric – ¼ tsp.
- Salt and ground black pepper, as required
- Medium head cauliflower – 1, cut into florets

Directions:
Add all the ingredients into a bowl and toss to coat well. Arrange the cauliflower florets onto a greased cooking tray. Arrange the drip pan in the bottom of the Instant Vortex Air Fryer Oven cooking chamber. Select "Bake" and then adjust the temperature to 450 °F. Set the time for 20 minutes and press "Start". When the display shows "Add Food" insert 1 tray in the top position and another in the bottom position. When the display shows "Turn Food" turn the cauliflower florets. When cooking time is complete, remove the tray from the Vortex Oven. Serve hot. Serve warm.

BROCCOLI BITES

Cooking Time: 12 minutes | Serves: 5

Ingredients:
- Broccoli florets – 1 cup
- Egg – 1, beaten
- Cheddar cheese – ¾ cup, grated
- Parmesan cheese – 2 tbsps. grated
- Panko breadcrumbs – ¾ cup
- Salt and ground black pepper, as required

Directions:

In a food processor, add the broccoli and pulse until finely crumbled. In a large bowl, mix together the broccoli, and remaining ingredients. Make small equal-sized balls from the mixture. Arrange the broccoli balls onto a greased cooking tray. Arrange the drip pan in the bottom of the Instant Vortex Air Fryer Oven cooking chamber. Select "Air Fry" and then adjust the temperature to 350 °F. Set the time for 12 minutes and press "Start". When the display shows "Add Food" insert the cooking tray in the center position. When the display shows "Turn Food" do not turn food. When cooking time is complete, remove the tray from the Vortex Oven. Serve warm.

CHICKEN NUGGETS

Cooking Time: 10 minutes | Serves: 6

Ingredients:
- Large chicken breasts – 2, cut into 1-inch cubes
- Breadcrumbs – 1 cup
- Parmesan cheese – 1/3 tbsp. shredded
- Onion powder – 1 tsp.
- Smoked paprika – ¼ tsp.
- Salt and ground black pepper, as required

Directions:
In a large resealable bag, add all ingredients. Seal the bag and shake well to coat completely. Arrange the nuggets onto a greased cooking tray. Arrange the drip pan in the bottom of the Instant Vortex Air Fryer Oven cooking chamber. Select "Air Fry" and then adjust the temperature to 400 °F. Set the time for 10 minutes and press "Start". When the display shows "Add Food" insert the cooking tray in the center position. When the display shows "Turn Food" turn the chicken nuggets. When cooking time is complete, remove the tray from the Vortex Oven. Serve warm.

SALMON CROQUETTES

Cooking Time: 7 minutes | Serves: 8

Ingredients:
- Half large can red salmon – drained
- Egg – 1, beaten lightly
- Fresh parsley – 1 tbsp. chopped
- Salt and ground black pepper, as required
- Vegetable oil – 3 tbsps.
- Breadcrumbs – ½ cup

Directions:

In a bowl, add the salmon and with a fork, mash it completely. Add the eggs, parsley, salt, and black pepper and mix until well combined. Make 8 equal-sized croquettes from the mixture. In a shallow dish, mix together the oil, and breadcrumbs. Coat the croquettes with the breadcrumb mixture. Arrange the croquettes onto a greased cooking tray. Arrange the drip pan in the bottom of the Instant Vortex Air Fryer Oven cooking chamber. Select "Air Fry" and then adjust the temperature to 390 °F. Set the time for 7 minutes and press "Start". When the display shows "Add Food" insert the cooking tray in the center position. When the display shows "Turn Food" turn the salmon croquettes. When cooking time is complete, remove the tray from the Vortex Oven. Serve warm.

BEEF TAQUITOS

Cooking Time: 8 minutes | Serves:

Ingredients:
- Corn tortillas – 6
- Cooked beef – 2 cups, shredded
- Onion – ½ cup, chopped
- Pepper Jack cheese – 1 cup, shredded
- Olive oil cooking spray

Directions:

Arrange the tortillas onto a smooth surface. Place the shredded meat over one corner of each tortilla, followed by onion and cheese. Roll each tortilla to secure the filling and secure with toothpicks. Spray each taquito with cooking spray evenly. Arrange the taquitos onto a cooking tray. Arrange the drip pan in the bottom of the Instant Vortex Air Fryer Oven cooking chamber. Select "Air Fry" and then adjust the temperature to 400 °F. Set the time for 8 minutes and press "Start". When the display shows "Add Food" insert the cooking tray in the center position. When the display shows "Turn Food" turn the taquitos. When cooking time is complete, remove the tray from the Vortex. Serve warm.

FISH AND SEAFOOD RECIPES

CRISPY TILAPIA

Cooking Time: 14 minutes | Serves: 4

Ingredients:
- Cornflakes – ¾ cup, crushed
- Dry ranch-style dressing mix – 1 (1-oz.) packet
- Vegetable oil – 2½ tbsps.
- Eggs – 2
- Tilapia fillets – 4 (6-oz.)

Directions:

In a shallow bowl, beat the eggs. In another bowl, add the cornflakes, ranch dressing, and oil and mix until a crumbly mixture forms. Dip the fish fillets into egg and then, coat with the cornflake mixture. Arrange the tilapia fillets onto the greased cooking tray. Arrange the drip pan in the bottom of the Instant Vortex Air Fryer Oven cooking chamber. Select "Air Fry" and then adjust the temperature to 355 °F. Set the time for 14 minutes and press "Start". When the display shows "Add Food" insert the cooking tray in the center position. When the display shows "Turn Food" turn the tilapia fillets. When cooking time is complete, remove the tray from the Vortex Oven. Serve hot.

SIMPLE HADDOCK

Cooking Time: 8 minutes | Serves: 2

Ingredients:
- Haddock fillets – 2 (6-oz.)
- Olive oil – 1 tbsp.
- Salt and ground black pepper, as required

Directions:
Coat the haddock fillets with oil and then, sprinkle with salt and black pepper. Arrange the haddock fillets onto a greased cooking rack and spray with cooking spray. Arrange the drip pan in the bottom of the Instant Vortex Air Fryer Oven cooking chamber. Select "Air Fry" and then adjust the temperature to 355 °F. Set the time for 8 minutes and press "Start". When the display shows "Add Food" insert the cooking rack in the center position. When the display shows "Turn Food" do not turn food. When the cooking time is complete, remove the rack from the Vortex Oven. Serve hot.

CRISPY HADDOCK

Cooking Time: 10 minutes | Serves: 3

Ingredients:
- Flour – ½ cup
- Paprika – ½ tsp.
- Egg – 1, beaten
- Mayonnaise – ¼ cup
- Salt and vinegar potato chips – 4 oz. crushed finely
- Haddock fillet – 1 lb. cut into 6 pieces

Directions:
In a shallow dish, mix together the flour and paprika. In a second shallow dish, add the egg and mayonnaise and beat well. In a third shallow dish, place the crushed potato chips. Coat the fish pieces with flour mixture, then dip into egg mixture and finally coat with the potato chips. Arrange the fish pieces onto 2 cooking trays. Arrange the drip pan in the bottom of the Instant Vortex Air Fryer Oven cooking chamber. Select "Air Fry" and then adjust the temperature to 370 °F. Set the time for 10 minutes and press "Start". When the display shows "Add Food" insert 1 cooking tray in the top position and another in the bottom position. When the display shows "Turn Food" do not turn the food but switch the position of cooking trays. When cooking time is complete, remove the trays from the Vortex Oven. Serve hot.

VINEGAR HALIBUT

Cooking Time: 12 minutes | Serves: 2

Ingredients:
- Halibut fillets – 2 (5-oz.)
- Garlic clove – 1, minced
- Fresh rosemary – 1 tsp. minced
- Olive oil – 1 tbsp.
- Red wine vinegar – 1 tbsp.
- Hot sauce – 1/8 tsp.

Directions:

In a large resealable bag, add all ingredients. Seal the bag and shale well to mix. Refrigerate to marinate for at least 30 minutes. Remove the fish fillets from the bag and shake off the excess marinade. Arrange the halibut fillets onto the greased cooking tray. Arrange the drip pan in the bottom of the Instant Vortex Air Fryer Oven cooking chamber. Select "Bake" and then adjust the temperature to 450 °F. Set the time for 12 minutes and press "Start". When the display shows "Add Food" insert the cooking tray in the center position. When the display shows "Turn Food" turn the halibut fillets. When the cooking time is complete, remove the tray from the Vortex Oven. Serve hot.

BREADED COD

Cooking Time: 10minutes | Serves: 4

Ingredients:
- All-purpose flour – 1/3 cup
- Ground black pepper, as required
- Egg – 1 large egg
- Water – 2 tbsps.
- Cornflakes – 2/3 cup, crushed
- Parmesan cheese – 1 tbsp. grated
- Cayenne pepper – 1/8 tsp.
- Cod fillets – 1 lb.
- Salt, as required

Directions:

In a shallow dish, add the flour and black pepper and mix well. In a second shallow dish, add the egg and water and beat well. In a third shallow dish, add the cornflakes, cheese and cayenne pepper and mix well. Season the cod fillets with salt evenly. Coat the fillets with flour mixture, then dip into egg mixture and finally coat with the cornflake mixture. Arrange the cod fillets onto the greased cooking rack. Arrange the drip pan in the bottom of the Instant Vortex Air Fryer Oven cooking chamber. Select "Air Fry" and then adjust the temperature to 400 °F. Set the time for 10 minutes and press "Start". When the display shows "Add Food" insert the cooking rack in the bottom position. When the display shows "Turn Food" turn the cod fillets. When cooking time is complete, remove the tray from the Vortex Oven. Serve hot.

SPICY CATFISH

Cooking Time: 14 minutes | Serves: 2

Ingredients:

- Cornmeal polenta – 2 tbsps.
- Cajun seasoning – 2 tsps.
- Paprika – ½ tsp.
- Garlic powder – ½ tsp.
- Salt, as required
- Catfish fillets – 2 (6-oz.)
- Olive oil – 1 tbsp.

Directions:

In a bowl, mix together the cornmeal, Cajun seasoning, paprika, garlic powder, and salt. Add the catfish fillets and coat evenly with the mixture. Now, coat each fillet with oil. Arrange the fish fillets onto a greased cooking rack and spray with cooking spray. Arrange the drip pan in the bottom of the Instant Vortex Air Fryer Oven cooking chamber. Select "Air Fry" and then adjust the temperature to 400 °F. Set the timer for 14 minutes and press "Start". When the display shows "Add Food" insert the cooking rack in the center position. When the display shows "Turn Food" turn the fillets. When cooking time is complete, remove the rack from the Vortex Oven. Serve hot.

TUNA BURGERS

Cooking Time: 6 minutes | Serves: 4

Ingredients:
- Canned tuna – 7 oz.
- Egg – 1 large
- Breadcrumbs – ¼ cup
- Mustard – 1 tbsp.
- Garlic powder – ¼ tsp.
- Onion powder – ¼ tsp.
- Cayenne pepper – ¼ tsp.
- Salt and ground black pepper, as required

Directions:

Add all the ingredients into a bowl and mix until well combined. Make 4 equal-sized patties from the mixture. Arrange the patties onto a greased cooking rack. Arrange the drip pan in the bottom of the Instant Vortex Air Fryer Oven cooking chamber. Select "Air Fry" and then adjust the temperature to 400 °F. Set the time for 6 minutes and press "Start". When the display shows "Add Food" insert the cooking rack in the center position. When the display shows "Turn Food" turn the burgers. When the cooking time is complete, remove the tray from the Vortex Oven. Serve hot.

CRAB CAKES

Cooking Time: 10 minutes | Serves: 4

Ingredients:
- Red bell pepper – ¼ cup, seeded and chopped finely
- Scallions – 2, chopped finely
- Mayonnaise – 2 tbsps.
- Breadcrumbs – 2 tbsps.
- Dijon mustard – 1 tbsp.
- Old bay seasoning – 1 tsp.
- lump crabmeat – 8 oz. drained

Directions:
Add all the ingredients into a bowl except the crabmeat and mix until thoroughly combined. Gently fold in the crabmeat. Make 4 equal-sized patties from the mixture. Arrange the patties onto a lightly greased cooking rack. Arrange the drip pan in the bottom of the Instant Vortex Air Fryer Oven cooking chamber. Select "Air Fry" and then adjust the temperature to 370 °F. Set the time for 10 minutes and press "Start". When the display shows "Add Food" insert the cooking rack in the center position. When the display shows "Turn Food" do not turn food. When the cooking time is complete, remove the tray from the Vortex Oven. Serve hot.

CRISPY PRAWNS

Cooking Time: 8 minutes | Serves: 4

Ingredients:
- Egg – 1
- Nacho chips – ½ lb. crushed
- Prawns – 12, peeled and deveined

Directions:
In a shallow dish, beat the egg. In another shallow dish, place the crushed nacho chips. Coat the prawn into egg and then roll into nacho chips. Arrange the coated prawns onto 2 cooking trays in a single layer. Arrange the drip pan in the bottom of the Instant Vortex Air Fryer Oven cooking chamber. Select "Air Fry" and then adjust the temperature to 355 °F. Set the time for 8 minutes and press "Start". When the display shows "Add Food" insert 1 tray in the top position and another in the bottom position. When the display shows "Turn Food" do not turn the food but switch the position of cooking trays. When cooking time is complete, remove the trays from the Vortex Oven. Serve hot.

PRAWNS IN BUTTER SAUCE

Cooking Time: 6 minutes | Serves: 2

Ingredients:
- Large prawns – ½ lb. peeled and deveined
- Large garlic clove – 1, minced
- Butter – 1 tbsp. melted
- Fresh lemon zest – 1 tsp. grated

Directions:
Add all the ingredients into a bowl and toss to coat well. Set aside at room temperature for about 30 minutes. Arrange the prawn mixture into a baking dish that will fit in the Vortex Air Fryer Oven. Arrange the drip pan in the bottom of the Instant Vortex Air Fryer Oven cooking chamber. Select "Bake" and then adjust the temperature to 450 °F. Set the time for 6 minutes and press "Start". When the display shows "Add Food" insert the baking dish in the center position. When cooking time is complete, remove the baking dish from the Vortex Oven. When the display shows "Turn Food" do not turn food. When cooking time is complete, remove the baking dish from the Vortex Oven. Serve hot.

LEMONY SHRIMP

Cooking Time: 8 minutes | Serves: 3

Ingredients:
- Fresh lemon juice – 2 tbsps.
- Olive oil – 1 tbsp.
- Lemon pepper – 1 tsp.
- Paprika – ¼ tsp.
- Garlic powder – ¼ tsp.
- Medium shrimp – 12 oz. peeled and deveined

Directions:

Add all the ingredients into a bowl except the shrimp and mix until well combined. Add the shrimp and toss to coat well. Arrange the shrimps onto a cooking rack. Arrange the drip pan in the bottom of the Instant Vortex Air Fryer Oven cooking chamber. Select "Air Fry" and then adjust the temperature to 400 °F. Set the time for 8 minutes and press "Start". When the display shows "Add Food" insert the cooking rack in the center position. When the display shows "Turn Food" do not turn food. When cooking time is complete, remove the tray from the Vortex Oven. Serve hot.

BREADED SHRIMP

Cooking Time: 12 minutes | Serves: 2

Ingredients:
- Large shrimp – 8, peeled and deveined
- Salt and ground black pepper, as required
- Coconut milk – 8 oz.
- Panko breadcrumbs – ½ cup
- Cayenne pepper – ½ tsp.

Directions:

In a shallow dish, mix together salt, black pepper and coconut milk. In another shallow dish, mix together breadcrumbs, cayenne pepper, salt and black pepper. Dip the shrimp in the coconut milk mixture and then roll into breadcrumbs mixture. Arrange the breaded shrimp onto the greased cooking tray in a single layer. Arrange the drip pan in the bottom of the Instant Vortex Air Fryer Oven cooking chamber. Select "Air Fry" and then adjust the temperature to 350 °F. Set the time for 12 minutes and press "Start". When the display shows "Add Food" insert the cooking tray in the center position. When the display shows "Turn Food" do not turn food. When cooking time is complete, remove the tray from the Vortex Oven. Serve hot.

COCONUT SHRIMP

Cooking Time: 12 minutes | Serves: 4

Ingredients:

- All-purpose flour – ½ cup
- Salt and ground white pepper, as required
- Egg whites – 2
- Plain breadcrumbs – ¾ cup
- Unsweetened coconut – ½ cup, shredded
- Lime zest – 2 tsps. grated finely
- Shrimp – 1 lb. peeled and deveined

Directions:

In a shallow dish, add the flour, salt and white pepper and mix well. In a second shallow dish, add the egg whites and beat lightly. In a third shallow dish, mix together the breadcrumbs, coconut and lime zest. Coat the shrimp with flour mixture, then dip into egg whites and finally coat with the coconut mixture. Arrange the coated shrimp onto 2 cooking trays in a single layer. Arrange the drip pan in the bottom of the Instant Vortex Air Fryer Oven cooking chamber. Select "Air Fry" and then adjust the temperature to 400 °F. Set the time for 12 minutes and press "Start". When the display shows "Add Food" insert 1 tray in the top position and another in the bottom position. When the display shows "Turn Food" do not turn the food but switch the position of cooking trays. When the cooking time is complete, remove the trays from the Vortex Oven. Serve hot.

BACON-WRAPPED SHRIMP

Cooking Time: 7 minutes | Serves: 6

Ingredients:
- Bacon – 1 lb. sliced thinly
- Shrimp – 1 lb. peeled and deveined

Directions:

Wrap one slice of bacon around each shrimp completely. Arrange the shrimp in a baking dish and refrigerate for about 20 minutes. Arrange the shrimp onto the greased cooking tray in a single layer. Arrange the drip pan in the bottom of the Instant Vortex Air Fryer Oven cooking chamber. Select "Air Fry" and then adjust the temperature to 390 °F. Set the time for 7 minutes and press "Start". When the display shows "Add Food" insert the cooking tray in the center position. When the display shows "Turn Food" do not turn food. When the cooking time is complete, remove the tray from the Vortex Oven. Serve hot.

POULTRY RECIPES

BBQ CHICKEN WINGS

Cooking Time: 19 minutes | Serves: 4

Ingredients:
- Chicken wings – 2 lb.
- Olive oil – 1 tsp.
- Smoked paprika – 1 tsp.
- Garlic powder – 1 tsp.
- Salt and ground black pepper, as required
- BBQ sauce – ¼ cup

Directions:
In a large bowl, mix together the chicken wings, smoked paprika, garlic powder, oil, salt, and pepper and mix well. Arrange the chicken wings onto the greased cooking tray. Arrange the drip pan in the bottom of Instant Vortex Air Fryer Oven cooking chamber. Select "Air Fry" and then adjust the temperature to 360 °F. Set the timer for 19 minutes and press "Start". When the display shows "Add Food" insert the cooking tray in the center position. When the display shows "Turn Food" turn the chicken wings and coat with BBQ sauce. When cooking time is complete, remove the trays from the Vortex Oven. Serve immediately.

BUFFALO CHICKEN WINGS

Cooking Time: 16 minutes | Serves: 5

Ingredients:
- Frozen chicken wings – 2 lb. drums and flats separated
- Olive oil – 2 tbsps.
- Buffalo sauce – 2 tbsps.
- Red pepper flakes – ½ tsp. crushed
- Salt, as required

Directions:

Coat the chicken wings with oil evenly. Arrange the chicken wings onto the greased cooking tray. Arrange the drip pan in the bottom of the Instant Vortex Air Fryer Oven cooking chamber. Select "Air Fry" and then adjust the temperature to 380 °F. Set the time for 25 minutes and press "Start". When the display shows "Add Food" insert the cooking tray in the center position. When the display shows "Turn Food" turn the chicken wings and coat with some Buffalo sauce. Meanwhile, in a large bowl, add the remaining Buffalo sauce, red pepper flakes and salt and mix well. When cooking time is complete, remove the trays from the Vortex Oven. Transfer the wings into the bowl of Buffalo sauce mixture and toss to coat well. Serve immediately.

PARMESAN CHICKEN TENDERS

Cooking Time: 15 minutes | Serves: 4

Ingredients:

- Flour – ½ cup
- Salt and ground black pepper, as required
- Eggs – 2, beaten
- Panko breadcrumbs – ¾ cup
- Parmesan cheese – ¾ cup, grated finely
- Italian seasoning – 1 tsp.
- Chicken tenders – 8

Directions:

In a shallow dish, place flour, salt and black pepper and mix well. In a second shallow dish, place the beaten eggs. In a third shallow dish, mix together the breadcrumbs, parmesan cheese and Italian seasoning. Coat the chicken tenders with flour mixture, then dip into the beaten eggs and finally coat with breadcrumb mixture. Arrange the tenders onto 2 greased cooking trays in a single layer. Arrange the drip pan in the bottom of the Instant Vortex Air Fryer Oven cooking chamber. Select "Air Fry" and then adjust the temperature to 360 °F. Set the time for 15 minutes and press "Start". When the display shows "Add Food" insert 1 tray in the top position and another in the bottom position. When the display shows "Turn Food" do not turn the food but switch the position of cooking trays. When cooking time is complete, remove the trays from the Vortex Oven. Serve hot.

SEASONED CHICKEN TENDERS

Cooking Time: 10 minutes | Serves: 2
Per Serves: Calories 220, Carbs 0.5g, Fat 8.4g, Protein 32.8g

Ingredients:
- Chicken tenders – 8 oz.
- BBQ seasoning – 1 tsp.
- Salt and ground black pepper, as required

Directions:

Season the chicken tenders with BBQ seasoning, salt and black pepper. Arrange the chicken tenders onto the greased cooking tray in a single layer. Arrange the drip pan in the bottom of the Instant Vortex Air Fryer Oven cooking chamber. Select "Bake" and then adjust the temperature to 450 °F. Set the time for 10 minutes and press "Start". When the display shows "Add Food" insert the rack in the center position. When the display shows "Turn Food" turn the chicken tenders. When cooking time is complete, remove the rack from the Vortex Oven. Serve hot.

CHICKEN CORDON BLEU

Cooking Time: 30 minutes | Serves: 2
Per Serves: Calories 672, Carbs 45.9g, Fat 28g, Protein 56.2g

Ingredients:
- Boneless, skinless chicken breast halves – 2 (6-oz.)
- Deli ham slices – 2 (¾-oz.)
- Swiss cheese slices – 2
- All-purpose flour – ½ cup
- Paprika – 1/8 tsp.
- Salt and ground black pepper, as required
- Large egg – 1
- 2% milk – 2 tbsps.
- Seasoned breadcrumbs – ½ cup
- Olive oil – 1 tbsp.
- Butter – 1 tbsp. melted

Directions:

Grease a baking dish that will fit in the Vortex Air Fryer Oven. With a meat mallet, pound each chicken breast half into ¼-inch thickness. Arrange the chicken breast halves onto a smooth surface. Arrange 1 ham slice over each chicken breast half, followed by the cheese. Roll up each chicken breast half and tuck in ends. With toothpicks, secure the rolls. In a shallow plate, mix together the flour, paprika, salt and black pepper. In a second shallow bowl, place the egg and milk and beat slightly. In a third shallow plate, place the breadcrumbs. Coat each chicken roll with flour mixture, then dip into egg mixture and finally coat with breadcrumbs. In a small skillet, heat the oil over a medium heat and cook the chicken rolls for about 3-5 minutes or until browned from all sides. Arrange the chicken rolls into the prepared baking dish. Arrange the drip pan in the bottom of the Instant Vortex Air Fryer Oven cooking chamber. Select "Bake" and then adjust the temperature to 350 °F. Set the time for 25 minutes and press "Start". When the display shows "Add Food" insert the baking dish in the center position. When the display shows "Turn Food" do not turn food. When the cooking time is complete, remove the baking dish from Vortex Oven. Discard the toothpicks from each chicken roll. Divide the chicken rolls onto serving plates and drizzle with melted butter. Serve immediately.

SIMPLE TURKEY BREAST

Cooking Time: 1 hour 20 minutes | Serves: 3

Ingredients:
- Bone-in, skin-on turkey breast half – 1 (2¾-lb.)
- Salt and ground black pepper, as required

Directions:
Rub the turkey breast with the salt and black pepper evenly. Arrange the turkey breast onto a greased cooking tray. Arrange the drip pan in the bottom of the Instant Vortex Air Fryer Oven cooking chamber. Select "Bake" and then adjust the temperature to 400 °F. Set the time for 1 hour 20 minutes and press "Start". When the display shows "Add Food" place the cooking tray over the drip pan. When the display shows "Turn Food" do not turn food. When the cooking time is complete, remove the cooking tray from the Vortex Oven. Place the turkey breast onto a cutting board. With a piece of foil, cover the turkey breast for about 20 minutes before slicing. With a sharp knife, cut the turkey breast into desired-sized slices and serve.

HERBED TURKEY BREAST

Cooking Time: 1 hour | Serves: 8

Ingredients:
- Olive oil – 2 tbsps.
- Fresh lemon juice – 2 tbsps.
- Garlic – 1 tbsp. minced
- Ground mustard – 2 tspa.
- Salt and ground black pepper, as required
- Ground sage – 1 tsp.
- Dried thyme – 1 tsp.
- Dried rosemary – 1 tsp.
- Turkey breast – 1 (3-lb.)

Directions:

In a small bowl, add all ingredients except the turkey breast and mix until well combined. Rub the oil mixture on the outside of the turkey breast and under any loose skin generously. Arrange the turkey breast onto the greased cooking tray, skin side up. Arrange the drip pan in the bottom of the Instant Vortex Air Fryer Oven cooking chamber. Select "Air Fry" and then adjust the temperature to 360 °F. Set the time for 60 minutes and press "Start". When the display shows "Add Food" insert the cooking tray in the center position. When cooking time is complete, press the red lever to release the rod. Remove from Vortex Oven and place the turkey breast onto a platter for about 5-10 minutes before slicing. With a sharp knife, cut the turkey breast into desired-sized slices and serve.

SPICED TURKEY BREAST

Cooking Time: 45 minutes | Serves: 8

Ingredients:
- Fresh rosemary – 2 tbsps. chopped
- Ground cumin – 1 tsp.
- Ground cinnamon – 1 tsp.
- Smoked paprika – 1 tsp.
- Cayenne pepper – 1 tsp.
- Salt and ground black pepper, as required
- Turkey breast – 1 (3-lb.)

Directions:
In a bowl, mix together the rosemary, spices, salt and black pepper. Rub the turkey breast with rosemary mixture evenly. With kitchen twines, tie the turkey breast to keep it compact. Arrange the turkey breast in the rotisserie basket and attach the lid. Arrange the drip pan in the bottom of Instant Vortex Air Fryer Oven cooking chamber. Select "Air Fry" and then adjust the temperature to 360 °F. Set the time for 45 minutes and press "Start". Then, close the door and touch "Rotate". When the display shows "Add Food" arrange the rotisserie basket, on the rotisserie spit. Then, close the door and touch "Rotate". When cooking time is complete, press the red lever to release the rod. Remove from Vortex Oven and place the turkey breast onto a platter for about 5-10 minutes before slicing. With a sharp knife, cut the turkey breast into desired-sized slices and serve.

HERBED DUCK BREAST

Cooking Time: 20 minutes | Serves: 2

Ingredients:
- Beer – 1 cup
- Olive oil – 1 tbsp.
- Mustard – 1 tsp.
- Fresh thyme – 1 tbsp. chopped
- Salt and ground black pepper, as required
- Duck breast – 1 (10½-oz.)

Directions:

In a bowl, add the beer, oil, mustard, thyme, salt, and black pepper and mix well. Add the duck breast and coat with the marinade generously. Cover the bowl and refrigerate for about 4 hours. Arrange the duck breast onto the greased cooking tray. Arrange the drip pan in the bottom of the Instant Vortex Air Fryer Oven cooking chamber. Select "Air Fry" and then adjust the temperature to 390 °F. Set the time for 20 minutes and press "Start". When the display shows "Add Food" insert the cooking tray in the center position. When the display shows "Turn Food" turn the duck breast. When cooking time is complete, remove the tray from the Vortex Oven. Place the duck breast onto a cutting board for about 5 minutes before slicing. With a sharp knife, cut the duck breast into desired-sized slices and serve.

GARLICKY DUCK LEGS

Cooking Time: 30 minutes | Serves: 2

Ingredients:
- Garlic cloves – 2, minced
- Fresh parsley – 1 tbsp. chopped
- Five-spice powder – 1 tsp.
- Salt and ground black pepper, as required
- Duck legs – 2

Directions:
In a bowl, mix together the garlic, parsley, five-spice powder, salt and black pepper. Rub the duck legs with garlic mixture generously. Arrange the duck legs onto the greased cooking tray. Arrange the drip pan in the bottom of the Instant Vortex Air Fryer Oven cooking chamber. Select "Air Fry" and then adjust the temperature to 340 °F. Set the time for 30 minutes and press "Start". When the display shows "Add Food" insert the cooking tray in the center position. When the display shows "Turn Food" turn the duck legs. When cooking time is complete, remove the tray from the Vortex Oven. Serve hot.

CHICKEN WITH AVOCADO & RADISH BOWL

Cooking Time: 20 minutes | Serves: 2

Ingredients:
- 12 oz chicken breasts
- 1 avocado, sliced
- 4 radishes, sliced
- 1 tbsp chopped parsley
- Salt and black pepper to taste

Directions:
Preheat the Air fryer to 300 F, and cut the chicken into small cubes. Combine all ingredients in a bowl and transfer to a baking dish. Cook for 14 minutes. Serve with cooked rice or fried red kidney beans.

SAVORY CHICKEN WITH ONION

Cooking Time: 20 minutes | Serves: 4

Ingredients:
- 4 chicken breasts, cubed
- 1 ½ cup onion soup mix
- 1 cup mushroom soup
- ½ cup cream

Directions:
Preheat your Fryer to 400 F. Add mushrooms, onion mix and cream in a frying pan. Heat on low heat for 1 minute. Pour the warm mixture over chicken slices and allow to sit for 25 minutes. Place the marinated chicken in the Air Fryer cooking basket and cook for 15 minutes. Serve with remaining cream and enjoy!

SAVORY BUFFALO CHICKEN

Cooking Time: 35 minutes | Serves: 4

Ingredients:
- 4 pounds chicken wing
- ½ cup cayenne pepper sauce
- ½ cup coconut oil
- 1 tbsp Worcestershire sauce
- 1 tbsp kosher salt

Directions:
1. In a mixing cup, combine cayenne pepper sauce, coconut oil, Worcestershire sauce and salt; set aside. Pat the chicken dry and place in the Air Fryer cooking basket. Cook for 25 minutes at 380 F.
2. Increase the temperature to 400 F and cook for 5 more minutes. Transfer into a large sized mixing bowl and toss in the prepared sauce. Serve with celery sticks and enjoy!

BASIL CHEESE CHICKEN

Cooking Time: 20 minutes | Serves: 4

Ingredients:
- 4 chicken breasts, cubed
- 1 tbsp garlic powder
- 1 cup mayonnaise
- ½ tsp pepper
- ½ cup soft cheese
- ½ tbsp salt
- Chopped basil for garnish

Directions:
Preheat your Air Fryer to 380 F. In a bowl, mix cheese, mayonnaise, garlic powder and salt to form a marinade. Cover your chicken with the marinade. Place the marinated chicken in your Air Fryer's cooking basket and cook for 15 minutes. Serve with a garnish of chopped basil.

MEAT RECIPES

BACON WRAPPED FILET MIGNON

Cooking Time: 15 minutes | Serves: 2

Ingredients:
- Bacon slices – 2
- Filet mignon – 2 (4-oz.)
- Salt and ground black pepper, as required
- Olive oil cooking spray

Directions:
Wrap 1 bacon slice around each filet mignon and secure with toothpicks. Season the filets with the salt and black pepper lightly. Arrange the filet mignon onto a cooking rack and spray with cooking spray. Arrange the drip pan in the bottom of the Instant Vortex Air Fryer Oven cooking chamber. Select "Air Fry" and then adjust the temperature to 375 °F. Set the time for 15 minutes and press "Start". When the display shows "Add Food" insert the cooking rack in the center position. When the display shows "Turn Food" turn the filets. When cooking time is complete, remove the rack from the Vortex Oven. Serve hot.

BEEF JERKY

Cooking Time: 3 hours | Serves: 4

Ingredients:
- Beef round – 1½ lbs. trimmed
- Worcestershire sauce – ½ cup
- Low-sodium soy sauce – ½ cup
- Honey – 2 tsps.
- Liquid smoke – 1 tsp.
- Onion powder – 2 tsps.
- Red pepper flakes – ½ tsp. crushed
- Ground black pepper, as required

Directions:
In a zip-top bag, place the beef and freeze for 1-2 hours to firm up. Place the meat onto a cutting board and cut against the grain into 1/8-¼-inch strips. In a large bowl, add the remaining ingredients and mix until thoroughly combined. Add the steak slices and coat with the mixture generously. Refrigerate to marinate for about 4-6 hours. Remove the beef slices from bowl and with paper towels, pat dry them. Divide the steak strips onto the cooking trays and arrange in an even layer. Arrange the drip pan in the bottom of the Instant Vortex Air Fryer Oven cooking chamber. Select "Dehydrate" and then adjust the temperature to 160 °F. Set the time for 3 hours and press "Start". When the display shows "Add Food" insert 1 tray in the top position and another in the center position. After 1½ hours, switch the position of cooking trays. When cooking time is complete, remove the trays from the Vortex Oven.

MEATBALLS

Cooking Time: 30 minutes | Serves: 8

Ingredients:

For Meatballs:
- Lean ground beef – 2 lb.
- Quick-cooking oats – 2/3 cup
- Ritz crackers – ½ cup, crushed
- Evaporated milk – 1 (5-oz.) can
- Large eggs – 2, beaten lightly
- Honey – 1 tsp.
- Dried onion – 1 tbsp. minced
- Garlic powder – 1 tsp.
- Ground cumin – 1 tsp.
- Salt and ground black pepper, as required

For Sauce:
- Orange marmalade – 1/3 cup
- Honey – 1/3 cup
- Brown sugar – 1/3 cup
- Cornstarch – 2 tbsps.
- Soy sauce – 2 tbsps.
- Hot sauce – 1-2 tbsps.
- Worcestershire sauce – 1 tbsp.

Directions:

For meatballs: Add all the meatball ingredients into a bowl and mix until thoroughly combined. Make 1½-inch balls from the mixture. Arrange half of the meatballs onto the greased cooking tray in a single layer. Arrange the drip pan in the bottom of the Instant Vortex Air Fryer Oven cooking chamber. Select "Air Fry" and then adjust the temperature to 380 °F. Set the time for 15 minutes and press "Start". When the display shows "Add Food" insert the cooking tray in the center position. When the display shows "Turn Food" turn the meatballs. When cooking time is complete, remove the tray from the Vortex Oven. Repeat with the remaining meatballs. Meanwhile, for sauce: in a small pan, add all ingredients over medium heat and cook until thickened, stirring continuously. Serve the meatballs with the topping of sauce.

BEEF BURGERS

Cooking Time: 18 minutes | Serves: 4

Ingredients:

For Burgers:
- Ground beef – 1 lb.
- Panko breadcrumbs – ½ cup
- Onion – ¼ cup, chopped finely
- Dijon mustard – 3 tbsps.
- Low-sodium soy sauce – 3 tsps.
- Fresh rosemary – 2 tsps. minced
- Salt, as required

For Topping:
- Dijon mustard – 2 tbsps.
- Brown sugar – 1 tbsp.
- Soy sauce – 1 tsp.
- Gruyere cheese slices – 4

Directions:

Add all the burger ingredients into a bowl and mix until thoroughly combined. Make 4 equal-sized patties from the mixture. Arrange the patties onto the greased cooking tray. Arrange the drip pan in the bottom of the Instant Vortex Air Fryer Oven cooking chamber. Select "Air Fry" and then adjust the temperature to 370 °F. Set the time for 15 minutes and press "Start". When the display shows "Add Food" insert the cooking rack in the center position. When the display shows "Turn Food" turn the burgers. Meanwhile, for sauce: in a small bowl, add the mustard, brown sugar and soy sauce and mix well. When cooking time is complete, remove the tray from the Vortex Oven and coat the burgers with the sauce. Top each burger with 1 cheese slice. Return the tray to the cooking chamber and select "Broil". Set the time for 3 minutes and press "Start". When cooking time is complete, remove the tray from the Vortex Oven. Serve hot.

BEEF CASSEROLE

Cooking Time: 25 minutes | Serves: 6

Ingredients:
- Ground beef – 2 lbs.
- Taco seasoning – 2 tbsps.
- Cheddar cheese – 1 cup, shredded
- Cottage cheese – 1 cup
- Salsa – 1 cup

Directions:

In a bowl, add the beef and taco seasoning and mix well. Add the cheeses and salsa and stir to combine. Place the mixture into a baking dish that will fit in the Vortex Air Fryer Oven. Arrange the drip pan in the bottom of the Instant Vortex Air Fryer Oven cooking chamber. Select "Air Fry" and then adjust the temperature to 370 °F. Set the time for 25 minutes and press "Start". When the display shows "Add Food" insert the baking dish in the center position. When the display shows "Turn Food" do not turn food. When the cooking time is complete, remove the baking dish from the Vortex Oven. Serve warm.

GARLICKY PORK TENDERLOIN

Cooking Time: 20 minutes | Serves: 5

Ingredients:
- Pork tenderloin – ½ lb.
- Nonstick cooking spray
- Small heads of roasted garlic – 2
- Salt and ground black pepper, as required

Directions:

Lightly, spray all the sides of pork with cooking spray and then, season with salt and black pepper. Now, rub the pork with roasted garlic. Arrange the roast onto the lightly greased cooking tray. Arrange the drip pan in the bottom of the Instant Vortex Air Fryer Oven cooking chamber. Select "Air Fry" and then adjust the temperature to 400 °F. Set the time for 20 minutes and press "Start". When the display shows "Add Food" insert the cooking tray in the center position. When the display shows "Turn Food" turn the pork. When cooking time is complete, remove the tray from the Vortex Oven. Place the roast onto a platter for about 10 minutes before slicing. With a sharp knife, cut the roast into desired-sized slices and serve.

GLAZED PORK TENDERLOIN

Cooking Time: 20 minutes | Serves: 3

Ingredients:
- Pork tenderloin – 1 lb.
- Sriracha – 2 tbsps.
- Honey – 2 tbsps.
- Salt, as required

Directions:

Insert the rotisserie rod through the pork tenderloin. Insert the rotisserie forks, one on each side of the rod to secure the pork tenderloin. In a small bowl, add the Sriracha, honey and salt and mix well. Brush the pork tenderloin with honey mixture evenly. Arrange the drip pan in the bottom of the Instant Vortex Air Fryer Oven cooking chamber. Select "Air Fry" and then adjust the temperature to 350 °F. Set the timer for 20 minutes and press "Start".When the display shows "Add Food" press the red lever down and load the left side of the rod into the Vortex. Now, slide the rod's left side into the groove along the metal bar so it doesn't move. Then, close the door and touch "Rotate". When cooking time is complete, press the red lever to release the rod. Remove the pork from the Vortex and place onto a platter for about 10 minutes before slicing. With a sharp knife, cut the roast into desired-sized slices and serve.

BUTTERED PORK LOIN

Cooking Time: 30 minutes | Serves: 6

Ingredients:
- Pork loin – 2 lb.
- Butter – 3 tbsps. melted and divided
- Salt and ground black pepper, as required

Directions:

Arrange a wire rack in a baking dish that will fit in the Vortex Air Fryer Oven. Coat the pork loin with melted butter evenly and then, rub with salt and black pepper generously. Arrange the pork loin into the prepared baking dish. Arrange the drip pan in the bottom of the Instant Vortex Air Fryer Oven cooking chamber. Select "Air Fry" and then adjust the temperature to 350 °F. Set the time for 30 minutes and press "Start". When the display shows "Add Food" insert the cooking rack in the center position. When the display shows "Turn Food" do not turn food. When cooking time is complete, remove the tray from the Vortex Oven. Place the pork loin onto a cutting board. With a piece of foil, cover the pork loin for about 10 minutes before slicing. With a sharp knife, cut the pork loin into desired-sized slices and serve.

SPICY PORK SHOULDER

Cooking Time: 55 minutes | Serves: 6

Ingredients:
- Ground cumin – 1 tsp.
- Cayenne pepper – 1 tsp.
- Garlic powder – 1 tsp.
- Salt and ground black pepper, as required
- Skin-on pork shoulder – 2 lbs.

Directions:
In a small bowl, place spices, salt and black pepper and mix well. Arrange the pork shoulder onto a cutting board, skin-side down. Season the inner side of the pork shoulder with salt and black pepper. With kitchen twines, tie the pork shoulder into a long round cylinder shape. Season the outer side of the pork shoulder with the spice mixture. Insert the rotisserie rod through the pork shoulder. Insert the rotisserie forks, one on each side of the rod to secure the pork shoulder. Arrange the drip pan in the bottom of the Instant Vortex Air Fryer Oven cooking chamber. Select "Roast" and then adjust the temperature to 350 °F. Set the time for 55 minutes and press "Start". When the display shows "Add Food" press the red lever down and load the left side of the rod into the Vortex. Now, slide the rod's left side into the groove along the metal bar so it doesn't move. Then, close the door and touch "Rotate". When cooking time is complete, press the red lever to release the rod. Remove the pork from the Vortex Oven and place onto a platter for about 10 minutes before slicing. With a sharp knife, cut the pork shoulder into desired-sized slices and serve.

BBQ PORK RIBS

Cooking Time: 26 minutes | Serves: 4

Ingredients:

- Honey – ¼ cup, divided
- BBQ sauce – ¾ cup
- Tomato ketchup – 2 tbsps.
- Worcestershire sauce – 1 tbsp.
- Soy sauce – 1 tbsp.
- Garlic powder – ½ tsp.
- Ground white pepper, as required
- Pork ribs – 1¾ lbs.

Directions:

In a bowl, mix together 3 tbsps. of honey and the remaining ingredients except the pork ribs. Add the pork ribs and coat with the mixture generously. Refrigerate to marinate for about 20 minutes. Arrange the ribs onto the greased cooking tray. Arrange the drip pan in the bottom of the Instant Vortex Air Fryer Oven cooking chamber. Select "Air Fry" and then adjust the temperature to 355 °F. Set the time for 26 minutes and press "Start". When the display shows "Add Food" insert the cooking tray in the center position. When the display shows "Turn Food" turn the ribs. When cooking time is complete, remove the tray from the Vortex Oven. Transfer the ribs onto serving plates. Drizzle with the remaining honey and serve immediately.

SEASONED PORK CHOPS

Cooking Time: 28 minutes | Serves: 2

Ingredients:
- Boneless pork chops – 2 (5-oz.)
- Buttermilk – 1 cup
- Flour – ½ cup
- Garlic powder – 1 tsp.
- Salt and ground black pepper, as required
- Olive oil cooking spray

Directions:
In a bowl, place the chops and buttermilk and refrigerate, covered for about 12 hours. Remove the chops from the bowl of buttermilk, discarding the buttermilk. In a shallow dish, place flour, garlic powder, salt, and black pepper and mix well. Coat the chops with flour mixture generously. Place the pork chops onto the cooking tray and spray with the cooking spray. Arrange the drip pan in the bottom of the Instant Vortex Air Fryer Oven cooking chamber. Select "Air Fry" and then adjust the temperature to 380 °F. Set the time for 28 minutes and press "Start". When the display shows "Add Food" insert the cooking tray in the center position. When the display shows "Turn Food" turn the pork chops. When cooking time is complete, remove the tray from the Vortex Oven. Serve hot.

GLAZED HAM

Cooking Time: 40 minutes | Serves: 4

Ingredients:
- Ham – 1 lb. 10½ oz.
- Whiskey – 1 cup
- French mustard – 2 tbsps.
- Honey – 2 tbsps.

Directions:

Place the ham at room temperature for about 30 minutes before cooking. Grease a baking dish that will fit in the Vortex Air Fryer Oven. In a bowl, mix together the whiskey, mustard, and honey. Place the ham in the prepared baking dish with half of the honey mixture and coat well. Arrange the drip pan in the bottom of the Instant Vortex Air Fryer Oven cooking chamber. Select "Air Fry" and then adjust the temperature to 320 °F. Set the time for 40 minutes and press "Start". When the display shows "Add Food" insert the baking dish in the center position. When cooking time is complete, remove the baking dish from the Vortex Oven. When the display shows "Turn Food" turn the ham and top with the remaining honey mixture. When cooking time is complete, remove the baking dish from the Vortex Oven. Place the ham onto a platter for about 10 minutes before slicing. Cut the ham into desired-sized slices and serve.

CRUSTED RACK OF LAMB

Cooking Time: 19 minutes | Serves: 4

Ingredients:

- Rack of lamb – 1, trimmed and frenched
- Salt and ground black pepper, as required
- Pistachios – 1/3 cup, chopped finely
- Panko breadcrumbs – 2 tbsps.
- Fresh thyme – 2 tsps. chopped
- Fresh rosemary – 1 tsp. chopped
- Butter – 1 tbsp. melted
- Dijon mustard – 1 tbsp.

Directions:

Insert the rotisserie rod through the rack on the meaty side of the ribs, right next to the bone. Insert the rotisserie forks, one on each side of the rod to secure the rack. Season the rack with salt and black pepper evenly. Arrange the drip pan in the bottom of the Instant Vortex Air Fryer Oven cooking chamber. Select "Air Fry" and then adjust the temperature to 380 °F. Set the time for 12 minutes and press "Start". When the display shows "Add Food" press the red lever down and load the left side of the rod into the Vortex. Now, slide the rod's left side into the groove along the metal bar so it doesn't move. Then, close the door and touch "Rotate". Meanwhile, in a small bowl, mix together the remaining ingredients except the mustard. When cooking time is complete, press the red lever to release the rod. Remove the the rack from Vortex Oven and brush the meaty side with the mustard. Then, coat the pistachio mixture on all sides of the rack and press firmly. Now, place the rack of lamb onto the cooking tray, meat side up. Select "Air Fry" and adjust the temperature to 380 °F. Set the time for 7 minutes and press "Start". When the display shows "Add Food" insert the cooking tray in the center position. When the display shows "Turn Food" do not turn food. When cooking time is complete, remove the tray from the Vortex Oven. Place the rack onto a cutting board for at least 10 minutes. Cut the rack into individual chops and serve.

LEMONY LAMB CHOPS

Cooking Time: 15 minutes | Serves: 2

Ingredients:
- Dijon mustard – 1 tbsp.
- Fresh lemon juice – ½ tbsp.
- Olive oil – ½ tsp.
- Dried tarragon – ½ tsp.
- Salt and ground black pepper, as required
- Lamb loin chops – 4 (4-oz.)

Directions:
In a large bowl, mix together the mustard, lemon juice, oil, tarragon, salt, and black pepper. Add the chops and coat with the mixture generously. Arrange the chops onto the greased cooking tray. Arrange the drip pan in the bottom of the Instant Vortex Air Fryer Oven cooking chamber. Select "Bake" and then adjust the temperature to 390 °F. Set the time for 15 minutes and press "Start". When the display shows "Add Food" insert the cooking tray in the center position. When the display shows "Turn Food" turn the chops. When cooking time is complete, remove the tray from the Vortex Oven. Serve hot.

HERBED LAMB CHOPS

Cooking Time: 11 minutes | Serves: 2

Ingredients:
- Lamb loin chops – 4 (4-oz.) (½-inch thick)
- Fresh rosemary – 2 tsps. minced
- Garlic cloves – 4, crushed
- Red chili powder – ¼ tsp.
- Salt and ground black pepper, as required

Directions:

In a large bowl, place all ingredients and mix well. Refrigerate to marinate overnight. Arrange the chops onto the greased cooking tray. Arrange the drip pan in the bottom of the Instant Vortex Air Fryer Oven cooking chamber. Select "Bake" and then adjust the temperature to 400 °F. Set the time for 11 minutes and press "Start". When the display shows "Add Food" insert the cooking tray in the center position. When the display shows "Turn Food" turn the chops. When cooking time is complete, remove the tray from the Vortex Oven. Serve hot.

BEEF BURGERS WITH PARSLEY & OREGANO

Cooking Time: 20 minutes | Serves: 4

Ingredients:
- 1 lb ground beef
- ½ tsp onion powder
- ½ tsp salt
- ½ tsp oregano
- 1 tbsp Worcestershire sauce
- ½ tsp garlic powder
- ½ tsp pepper
- 1 tsp parsley
- 1 tsp maggi seasoning sauce
- 1 tsp olive oil

Directions:
1. Preheat the air fryer to 350 F. Combine all of the sauces and seasonings, except oil, in a small bowl. Place the beef in a bowl and stir in the seasonings. Mix until the mixture is well incorporated.
2. Divide the meat mixture into four equal pieces and form patties. Spread the olive oil in the air fryer. Arrange the 4 burgers inside and cook for 10 to 15 minutes, until thoroughly cooked.

BEEF WITH CAULIFLOWER AND GREEN PEAS

Cooking Time: 25 minutes | Serves: 4

Ingredients:
- 2 beef steaks, sliced into thin strips
- 2 garlic cloves, chopped
- 2 tsp maple syrup
- 1 tsp oyster sauce
- 1 tsp cayenne pepper
- ½ tsp olive oil
- Juice of 1 lime
- Salt and black pepper
- 1 cauliflower, cut into florets
- 2 carrots, cut into chunks
- 1 cup green peas

Directions:
In a bowl, add beef, garlic, maple syrup, oyster sauce, cayenne, oil, lime juice, salt, and black pepper, and stir to combine. Place the beef along with the garlic and some of the juices into your air fryer and top with the veggies. Cook at 400 F for 8 minutes, turning once halfway through.

AWESOME RIB EYE STEAK

Cooking Time: 20 minutes | Serves: 6

Ingredients:
- 2 lb rib eye steak
- 1 tbsp. steak rub
- 1 tbsp. olive oil

Directions:
Preheat the fryer to 400 F. Combine the steak rub and olive oil. Rub the steak with the seasoning. Place in the air fryer and cook for 10 minutes. Flip the steak over and cook for 7 more minutes. Serve hot with potatoes.

DESSERTS RECIPES

APPLE PIE ROLLS

Cooking Time: 12 minutes | Serves: 4

Ingredients:
- Tart apples – 1½ cups, peeled, cored and chopped
- Light brown sugar – ¼ cup
- Ground cinnamon – 1¼ tsps. divided
- Corn starch – ½ tsp.
- Egg roll wrappers – 4
- Cream cheese – ¼ cup, softened
- Olive oil cooking spray
- Sugar – 1 tbsp.

Directions:

In a small bowl, mix together the apples, brown sugar, 1 tsp. of cinnamon and corn starch. Arrange 1 egg roll wrapper onto a smooth surface. Spread about 1 tbsp. of cream cheese over roll, leaving 1-inch of edges. Place 1/3 cup of apple mixture over one corner of a wrapper, just below the center. Fold the bottom corner over filling. With wet fingers, moisten the remaining wrapper edges. Fold side corners toward center over filling. Roll egg roll up tightly and with your fingers, press at tip to seal. Repeat with the remaining wrappers, cream cheese and filling. Arrange the rolls onto a cooking tray and spray with the cooking spray. Arrange the drip pan in the bottom of the Instant Vortex Air Fryer Oven cooking chamber. Select "Air Fry" and then adjust the temperature to 400 °F. Set the time for 12 minutes and press "Start".When the display shows "Add Food" insert the cooking tray in the center position. When the display shows "Turn Food" turn the rolls and spray with the cooking spray. Meanwhile, in a shallow dish, mix together the sugar and remaining cinnamon. When the cooking time is complete, remove the tray from the Vortex. Coat the hot egg rolls with the sugar mixture and serve.

BERRY TACOS

Cooking Time: 5 minutes | Serves: 2

Ingredients:
- Soft shell tortillas – 2
- Strawberry jelly – 4 tbsps.
- Fresh blueberries – ¼ cup
- Fresh raspberries – ¼ cup
- Powdered sugar – 2 tbsps.

Directions:

Spread 2 tbsps. of strawberry jelly over each tortilla. Top each with berries evenly and sprinkle with powdered sugar. Arrange the tortillas onto a greased cooking rack. Arrange the drip pan in the bottom of the Instant Vortex Air Fryer Oven cooking chamber. Select "Air Fry" and then adjust the temperature to 300 °F. Set the timer for 5 minutes and press "Start". When the display shows "Add Food" insert the cooking rack in the center position. When the display shows "Turn Food" do not turn food. When cooking time is complete, remove the rack from the Vortex Oven. Place the tortillas aside to cool slightly. Serve warm.

CINNAMON DONUTS

Cooking Time: 12 minutes | Serves: 8

Ingredients:
- Granulated sugar – ½ cup
- Ground cinnamon – 1 tbsp.
- Flaky large biscuits – 1 (16.3-oz.) can
- Olive oil cooking spray
- Unsalted butter – 4 tbsps. melted

Directions:

Line a baking sheet with parchment paper. In a shallow dish, mix together the sugar and cinnamon. Set aside. Remove the biscuits from the can and carefully, separate them. Place the biscuits onto the prepared baking sheet and with a 1-inch round biscuit cutter, cut holes from the center of each biscuit. Place 4 donuts onto the lightly greased cooking tray in a single layer. Arrange the drip pan in the bottom of the Instant Vortex Air Fryer Oven cooking chamber. Select "Air Fry" and then adjust the temperature to 350 °F. Set the time for 6 minutes and press "Start". When the display shows "Add Food" insert the cooking tray in the center position. When the display shows "Turn Food" turn the donuts. When cooking time is complete, remove the tray from the Vortex. Brush both sides of the warm donuts with melted butter and then, coat with cinnamon sugar. Repeat with the remaining donuts. Serve warm.

CHOCOLATE CUPCAKES

Cooking Time: 15 minutes | Serves: 6

Ingredients:

- All-purpose flour – 1 cup
- Unsweetened cocoa powder – 2 tbsps.
- Baking soda – ¼ tsp.
- Baking powder – 1 tsp.
- Salt – ¼ tsp.
- Coconut milk – ½ cup
- Granulated sugar – ¼ cup
- Coconut oil – 3 tbsps. melted
- Vanilla extract – ½ tsp.
- Dark chocolate chips – ½ cup
- Pistachios – ¼ cup, chopped

Directions:

Place the flour, cocoa powder, baking powder, baking soda, and salt into a bowl and mix thoroughly. Place the coconut milk, sugar, coconut oil and vanilla extract into another bowl and beat until thoroughly combined. Add in the flour mixture and mix until just combined. Fold in the chocolate chips and pistachios. Grease a 6 cup muffin pan. Place the mixture into prepared muffin cups about ¾ full. Arrange the muffin pan on top of a cooking rack. Arrange the drip pan in the bottom of the Instant Vortex Air Fryer Oven cooking chamber. Select "Air Fry" and then adjust the temperature to 300°F. Set the time for 15 minutes and press "Start". When the display shows "Add Food" insert the cooking rack in the center position. When the display shows "Turn Food" do not turn food. When cooking time is complete, remove the ramekins from the Vortex Oven. Place the muffin pan onto a wire rack" to cool for 10-15 minutes. Carefully, invert the muffins onto the wire rack to cool completely before serving.

BANANA MUG CAKE

Cooking Time: 30 minutes
Serve: 1Protein 6.9g

Ingredients:
- All-purpose flour – ¼ cup
- Ground cinnamon – 1/8 tsp.
- Baking soda – ¼ tsp.
- Salt – 1/8 tsp.
- Banana – ½ cup, peeled and mashed
- Sugar – 2 tbsps.
- Butter – 1 tbsp. melted
- Egg yolk – 1
- Vanilla extract – ¼ tsp.

Directions:

In a bowl, mix together the flour, baking soda, cinnamon and salt. In another bowl, add the mashed banana and sugar and beat well. Add the butter, the egg yolk, and the vanilla and mix well. Add the flour mixture and mix until just combined. Place the mixture into a lightly greased ramekin. Arrange the ramekin on top of a cooking rack. Arrange the drip pan in the bottom of the Instant Vortex Air Fryer Oven cooking chamber. Select "Air Fry" and then adjust the temperature to 350 °F. Set the time for 30 minutes and press "Start". When the display shows "Add Food" insert the cooking rack in the center position. When the display shows "Turn Food" do not turn food. When cooking time is complete, remove the ramekin from the Vortex Oven. Place the ramekin onto a wire rack to cool slightly before serving.

RUM CAKE

Cooking Time: 25 minutes | Serves: 6

Ingredients:
- Yellow cake mix – ½ package
- Jell-O instant pudding – ½ (3.4-oz.) package
- Eggs – 2
- Vegetable oil – ¼ cup
- Water – ¼ cup
- Dark rum – ¼ cup

Directions:
Add all the ingredients into a bowl and with an electric mixer, beat until thoroughly combined. Arrange a parchment paper in the bottom of a greased 8-inch cake pan. Now, arrange a foil piece around the cake pan. Place the mixture into the prepared cake pan and with the back of a spoon, smooth the top surface. Arrange the drip pan in the bottom of the Instant Vortex Air Fryer Oven cooking chamber. Select "Air Fry" and then adjust the temperature to 325 °F. Set the timer for 25 minutes and press "Start". When the display shows "Add Food" place the cake pan over the drip pan. When the display shows "Turn Food" do nothing. When the cooking time is complete, remove the pan from the Vortex and place onto a wire rack to cool for about 10 minutes. Carefully, invert the cake onto wire rack to cool completely before cutting. Cut into desired-sized slices and serve.

CHERRY CLAFOUTIS

Cooking Time: 25 minutes | Serves: 4

Ingredients:
- Fresh cherries – 1½ cups, pitted
- Vodka – 3 tbsps.
- Flour – ¼ cup
- Sugar – 2 tbsps.
- Pinch of salt
- Sour cream – ½ cup
- Egg – 1
- Butter – 1 tbsp.
- Powdered sugar – ¼ cup

Directions:

In a bowl, mix together the cherries and vodka. In another bowl, mix together the flour, sugar, and salt. Add the sour cream, and egg and mix until a smooth dough forms. Place flour mixture into a greased cake pan. Spread cherry mixture over the dough. Place butter on the top in the form of dots. Arrange the cake pan on top of a cooking rack. Arrange the drip pan in the bottom of the Instant Vortex Air Fryer Oven cooking chamber. Select "Air Fry" and then adjust the temperature to 355 °F. Set the time for 25 minutes and press "Start". When the display shows "Add Food" insert the cooking rack in the center position. When the display shows "Turn Food" do not turn food. When cooking time is complete, remove the ramekins from the Vortex Oven. Place the cake pan onto a wire rack to cool for about 10-15 minutes before serving. Now, invert the Clafoutis onto a platter and sprinkle with powdered sugar. Cut the Clafoutis into desired-sized slices and serve warm.

BLUEBERRY COBBLER

Cooking Time: 20 minutes | Serves: 6

Ingredients:

For Filling:
- Fresh blueberries – 2½ cups
- Vanilla extract – 1 tsp.
- Fresh lemon juice – 1 tsp.
- Sugar – 1 cup
- Flour – 1 tsp.
- Butter – 1 tbsp. melted

For Topping:
- All-purpose flour – 1¾ cups
- Sugar – 6 tbsps.
- Baking powder – 4 tsps.
- Milk – 1 cup
- Butter – 5 tbsps. butter

For Sprinkling:
- Sugar – 2 tsps.
- Ground cinnamon – ¼ tsp.

Directions:

For filling: Add all the ingredients into a bowl and mix until thoroughly combined. For topping: in another large bowl, mix together the flour, baking powder, and sugar. Add the milk and butter and mix until a crumbly mixture forms. For sprinkling: in a small bowl mix together the sugar and cinnamon. In the bottom of a greased baking pan, place the blueberries mixture and top with the flour mixture evenly. Sprinkle the cinnamon sugar on top evenly. Arrange the drip pan in the bottom of the Instant Vortex Air Fryer Oven cooking chamber. Select "Air Fry" and then adjust the temperature to 320 °F. Set the time for 20 minutes and press "Start". When the display shows "Add Food" place the baking dish over the drip pan. When the display shows "Turn Food" do not turn food. When cooking time is complete, remove the pan from the Vortex Oven. Place the baking pan onto a wire rack to cool for about 10 minutes before serving. Cut into desired-sized slices and serve.

APPLE CRUMBLE

Cooking Time: 25 minutes | Serves: 4

Ingredients:
- apple pie filling – 1 (14-oz.) can
- Butter – ¼ cup, softened
- Self-raising flour – 9 tbsps.
- Caster sugar – 7 tbsps.
- Pinch of salt

Directions:

Lightly, grease a baking dish that will fit in the Vortex Air Fryer Oven. Place apple pie filling into the prepared baking dish evenly. In a medium bowl, add the remaining ingredients and mix until a crumbly mixture forms. Spread the mixture over apple pie filling evenly. Arrange the baking dish on top of a cooking rack. Arrange the drip pan in the bottom of the Instant Vortex Air Fryer Oven cooking chamber. Select "Air Fry" and then adjust the temperature to 320 °F. Set the time for 25 minutes and press "Start". When the display shows "Add Food" insert the cooking rack in the center position. When the display shows "Turn Food" do not turn food. When cooking time is complete, remove the baking dish from the Vortex Oven. Place the baking dish onto a wire rack to cool for about 10 minutes. Serve warm.

STRAWBERRY CHEESECAKE

Cooking Time: 1 hour 37 minutes | Serves: 8

Ingredients:
For Crust:
- Almond flour – 7 tbsps.
- Natural peanut butter – 2 tbsps.
- Honey – 1 tbsp.

For Filling:
- Eggs – 2
- Plain Greek yogurt – 10½ oz.
- Cream cheese – 10½ oz.
- vanilla whey protein powder – 2 scoops
- Strawberry preserve – 2 tbsps.
- Splenda – 2 tbsps.
- Vanilla extract – ¼ tsp.
- Fresh strawberries – 1 cup, hulled and sliced

For Topping:
- Fat-free plain Greek yogurt – 2 tbsps.
- Splenda – 1 tbsp.
- Vanilla whey protein powder – 2 tbsps.

Directions:
With a parchment paper, line a greased round baking dish. For crust: Add the crust ingredients into a bowl and mix until a dough ball forms. Place the dough ball in the center of prepared baking dish. With your fingers, press downwards until the dough spreads evenly in the bottom of baking dish. Arrange the drip pan in the bottom of the Instant Vortex Air Fryer Oven cooking chamber. Select "Air Fry" and then adjust the temperature to 248 °F. Set the time for 7 minutes and press "Start". When the display shows "Add Food" place the baking dish over the drip pan. When the display shows "Turn Food" do not turn food. When the cooking time is complete, remove the baking dish from Vortex Oven. Place the crust onto a wire rack to cool slightly. Meanwhile, for filling: in a large bowl, put all the filling ingredients except strawberries and whisk until smooth. Fold in the strawberry slices. Place strawberry mixture over the crust evenly. With the back of spatula, smooth the top surface of strawberry mixture. Again, select "Air Fry" and then adjust the temperature to 248 °F. Set the time for 30 minutes and press "Start". When the display shows "Add Food" insert the baking dish in the center position. After 30 minutes, adjust the temperature to 195 °F. Set the time for 60 minutes. When the display shows "Turn Food" do not turn food. When the cooking time is complete, remove the baking dish from the Vortex Oven. Place the baking dish aside for about 1-2 hours to cool. For topping: in a bowl, put all the topping ingredients and mix well. After cooling, top the cheesecake with the topping mixture. Refrigerate for about 4-8 hours before serving.

VANILLA LEMON CHEESECAKE

Cooking Time: 80 minutes | Serves: 8

Ingredients:
- 8 oz graham crackers, crushed
- 4 oz butter, melted
- 16 oz plain cream cheese
- 3 eggs
- 3 tbsp sugar
- 1 tbsp vanilla extract
- Zest of 2 lemons

Directions:
Line a cake tin, that fits in your Air fryer, with baking paper. Mix together the crackers and butter, and press at the bottom of the tin. In a bowl, add cream cheese, eggs, sugar, vanilla and lemon zest and beat with a hand mixer until well combined and smooth. Pour the mixture into the tin, on top of the cracker's base. Cook for 40-45 minutes at 350 F, checking it to ensure it's set but still a bit wobbly. Let cool, then refrigerate overnight.

www.ingramcontent.com/pod-product-compliance
Lightning Source LLC
Chambersburg PA
CBHW081120080526
44587CB00021B/3679